I0425477

Self-Confidence Workbook

Cognitive Behavioral Therapy Guide for Men and Women to Overcoming Self-Doubt and Improve Self-Critic, Self-Esteem and Self-Confidence

Dr. Jake Sharp

Debut Bestselling Author

Table of Contents

Introduction

Our minds can get the best of us sometimes, which makes it difficult to be self-confident and self-reliant. We all have an inner critic that makes our minds overload with our faults or thoughts of the past and future. The inner critic is that silent voice that overloads us with negative thoughts, pressure, or beliefs, underestimating us and telling us that we can't do something. Having this inner voice can impair our ability to manage and deal with stress or other situations that life throws our way. When we continue to believe our inner critic for a long period of time, our self-esteem or self-image becomes distorted, which can cause high volumes of stress, resulting in depression or anxiety.

This confidence workbook has two parts. The first part explains the concepts of self-love, individuality, self-esteem, self-respect, and self-worth. You will learn why you don't feel confident and what patterns you have developed over time that get you where you are. This way, you will find a deeper understanding of yourself. By the time you get to the second part of this book, you will be ready to learn how to reverse your negativity and find inner peace. Everyone has self-confidence already programmed in them, but because of their minds falling short of the positive aspects in life, they forgot how to be confident and individualistic. One thing is for sure—we are all worthy and deserving of respect and appreciation.

Everywhere, you see books that have titles like *How to Practice Positivity* and *How to Be a Better You in These Simple Steps.* Everywhere you look, the media and entertainment centers are promoting personal growth. Much like this book, you can learn how to do anything and develop anything you want just by following the advice given. This book is different from the rest because it not only shows you how but also explains in detail why you got stuck and how to overcome it. Aside from the inner critic interrupting our growth, one thing that stops us is *fear*. People fear the unknown because it is uncertain what will happen. However, if you have self-confidence, you know what you deserve, and you trust yourself to move forward no matter what lies ahead. With the help of this book, you will learn how to overcome your fears, anxiety, and worries. It's time to open your mind to the possibility and opportunity of self-love and awareness.

There are many benefits to growing out of your shyness shell, building healthy relationships, creating plans, and learning how to trust yourself to build confidence. Why are you stuck? Have you always wanted to know where to begin picking yourself up? This book has the answers.

Ask yourself one question: "What makes life worth living?" It's personal growth. If you are not ready to commit to change, overcome your fears, and become satisfied in your own reality, then do not read any further. Put this book down and find something else to read. This book requires your full attention and your full dedication. Above all else, it provides you with well-researched information suited directly for your needs. Life is too short to waste your time on the inner critic who believes you should fail. So quit wasting time. Beat your shyness and become the confident individual you have always wanted to be.

Part One: Identifying Self-Confidence

In part one of this self-confidence workbook, there are three chapters that explain what self-confidence is and all the aspects surrounding self-esteem. You will understand yourself on a deeper level, and you will learn where self-confidence and self-esteem come from. You will learn that by giving yourself kindness, compassion, and love, your self-esteem level and confidence will rise. Have you ever wondered why you feel as though you are headed in the right path, then something knocks you down and you are three steps backward from where you were? This can happen because of low levels of confidence and self-esteem. Yes, they are different. As you learn how to implement self-respect into your life, you will start to see the triggers in your life that keep you from climbing the success ladder. With the power of positivity and using many ways to defeat that inner critical voice of yours, you can step out of the darkness and become the light of your own desire.

These next three chapters will give you a deeper definition of what self-confidence, self-love, self-respect, self-worth, self-esteem, and care are all about. Each one is unique in its own definition and ties together to make up what self-esteem and self-confidence are supposed to be. One thing is certain—you can never be confident with the ongoing critical voice that ties you down inside your head. So the first step is to overcome the "negative Nancy" and find a deeper meaning so that you can be motivated to live the life you deserve.

Chapter 1: Understanding Yourself

The most important step in building self-confidence and self-esteem is to understand first who you are. Believe it or not, there are a lot of people who don't understand who they are yet and struggle with the process of figuring it out. This chapter welcomes you to explore yourself and get to know who you are on a deeper level so that when you finally commit to personal growth, you can understand what works best for you and find ways to get what you want. Do you often wonder why you got upset for no reason? Maybe you don't enjoy your job but wonder why you stay. Have you ever argued with your spouse about things that seem unnecessary? A lot of our automatic reactions stem from our subconscious mind, which controls a large amount of our behavior. If you understand yourself better (what makes you do what you do and why you think the way you do), you can gain a better understanding of how to make better decisions, thus resulting in higher self-confidence.

There are a few steps in learning how to understand yourself better:

Get a Personal Assessment

You can ask a few of your friends and family members for their opinion of who they think you are, but this may lead to biases of yourself that you already have. Instead of asking around, you can take a few personality tests like the Myer-Briggs personality test, or you can research about the nine basic personality types through the enneagram test.

The Myers-Briggs personality test theory represents sixteen different personality types that you could fall under. Depending on your answers, the tests consist of eight different types of people you can be—introvert/extrovert, sensing/intuition, thinking/feeling, and judging/perceiving. The results would explain which of the sixteen personalities you fit into. For example, ENFJ would be that you would fall in to be an extrovert, intuitive, feeling, and judgmental person.

The enneagram test is a little more complicated and takes a bit to understand; however, it consists of nine different types of personalities that you fall into. It consists of a diagram that explains personal growth and where you are on the scale and how to get to where you want to be. The enneagram doesn't fit you into one specific category as it leaves room for you to grow into any personality type. As confusing as these tests may be, by researching and undergoing a personality test, you may be able to understand yourself a little deeper.

Do Individuality/Personality Writing Exercises

A character analysis writing activity is what fictional writers will do so that they have a better understanding of the characters they want to discuss in their books. You can find many templates online, and the goal of this project is to think about things you weren't aware of yourself. Some of the character outlines consist of asking whether a person has any habits or "ticks" that may separate them from the world, like nail-biting, or whether they have an accent. Below are some questions you can ask yourself:

1. How do you describe yourself?

2. What is your purpose?

3. What is the most important thing that has happened to you?

4. What is the most embarrassing thing that has happened to you?

5. What are you most interested in?

6. What do you value and appreciate the most?

7. What makes you different from other people?

8. What is one experience that was life-changing for you?

By answering these specific questions, you will gain a better understanding of who you are.

Define Your Strengths and Weaknesses

By evaluating and thinking solely about your strengths and weaknesses, you can figure out what is most important to you that will help you answer the questions you struggled with in your writing exercise. Compare your perception with your strengths and weaknesses to the strengths and weaknesses of your friends and family. This can help you understand more about yourself and how you see yourself and reflect.

Some examples of strengths are being devoted, dedicated, resilient, decisive, and organized. Some examples of weaknesses are being narrow-minded, selfish, unsure, and judgmental.

Evaluate Your Priorities and What's Important to You

Your priorities stem down to your beliefs, morals, and values. When you think about these things, you can determine what is most important to you. Here are a few things to consider when determining your priorities:

1. If your house is on fire, what is the first thing that comes to your mind that you will save? These can be anything from tax papers to memorabilia.

2. If someone is living a lifestyle that you don't agree with, like veganism or transsexualism (just an example), how would you respond? Even though you don't agree, would you still be supportive? Would you protect them? How?

3. What is most important to you? Some examples of things that people mostly prioritize are money, family, respect, and stability.

In understanding yourself on a deeper level, you will be able to experience more happiness and self-control. You will be able to make wiser decisions. You will have resilience during stressful events, and you will gain a deeper understanding of others. Many benefits come with understanding yourself. Now let us learn what self-confidence and self-esteem are.

Understanding Self-Confidence

By definition, "confidence" is a state in which someone feels a certain truth about something. Confidence is when someone can dive into something with pure trust that everything is going to be all right and perfect. It's the self-assurance of oneself that things will happen correctly. It's being 100% sure of yourself and your beliefs. This can fully happen when someone understands themselves and knows who they are as an individual. It is when someone feels good about themselves and trusts their capabilities fully. Self-confidence comes from three abilities that everyone possesses, which are as follows:

- the ability to think positively about yourself and your environment

- the ability to be completely certain that you implement positive value in your life and have trust in all your capabilities (regardless of what others feel and think of you)

- the ability to continue thinking positively about yourself and situations through any given circumstance (even when negativity arises)

So what do these abilities all have in common? They are all positive-based thinking patterns. So in order to be a self-confident individual, you must obtain absolute positivity while also knowing when to accept the negative.

A lot of people try to control what is impossible to control, like the future. When we are stuck trying to control the future, we are stuck focusing on the negative instead of accepting that it hasn't happened yet. Being confident is about knowing when to act upon things you can control and when to sit with things you can't.

One thing to keep in mind about self-confidence is that it is neither right nor wrong; however, it is very useful to have. Just as a glass that is full or empty is neither right nor wrong, if you lack self-confidence, that is neither right nor wrong as well. One of the most beneficial things about being confident is that through every experience, you get stronger and wiser rather than weaker and feeling stuck in the same place. By this, I mean, when you have low self-confidence, you are bound to feel rejected or judged, which makes situations more difficult to handle. With that being said, you may not be able to "put yourself out there for fear of being judged or rejected." In this sense, over time, you become weaker and weaker because you become more and more terrified to do the things you want. Because of low self-confidence, you wouldn't take risks needed to live a fulfilled and satisfying life.

Here are the benefits of having high self-confidence:

- more respect for yourself and your self-worth

- more happiness and appreciation

- less self-doubt

- less anxiety and fear

- less stress

- more energy and dedication to strive forward

- overall better physical and mental health

More benefits will be explained in more detail in chapter 3. When you have self-confidence, the petty stuff doesn't matter to you. You are not afraid of rejection or judgment because you know yourself. You have high self-respect, and someone else's opinion of you does not break your stride. If you want to learn how to build your self-esteem and be more self-confident as an individual, the second part of this book explains and teaches you how you can do this.

Understanding Self-Esteem

Self-esteem can be referred to as self-worth or self-respect. People with low self-esteem may feel defeated or maintain an overload of unnecessary stress, which leads them to make bad choices. Bad choices can lead someone to destructive relationships, poor performance at work, and decreased overall health. Although someone with low self-esteem can be dangerous. People who represent high levels of self-esteem are also at risk for harmful experiences. Self-esteem is about how you feel about yourself. How much do you like yourself, and what are you worth to yourself? These are good questions to ask when learning about self-esteem and how to develop the qualities. When you learn more about yourself (especially what helps you feel more confident and how much you deserve for yourself), you will learn not to accept anything less from anyone else. And when you can do that, you will develop stronger bonds with the people around you, put your best foot forward in everything you do, and be a much happier person overall.

Here are some signs that you have high self-esteem:

- You have confidence.

- You are able to say no.

- You have a positive mindset.

- You accept your own strengths and weaknesses.

- Negative experiences are not hugely impactful.

- You are able to express your needs and how you feel.

Here are signs that you have low self-esteem:

- You have a negative mindset.

- You lack confidence.

- Focus is always on the negative aspects of life.

- You feel ashamed, depressed, or fearful.

- You believe that other people are better than you.

- You feel envy or jealousy.

- You cannot accept compliments and are sensitive to any type of feedback.

- You fear failure, so you tend to be a perfectionist.

Confidence is one of the biggest traits when learning or developing self-esteem. Self-esteem is about self-love, and having too much of that can make you seem egotistical, entitled, narcissistic, and even arrogant. Not enough self-esteem can make someone more willing to tolerate less than they deserve and take on too much for their stress level. This is what we would call a pushover. The right amount of self-esteem can greatly benefit the way you work, the way you see the world, the way you interact with others, and the way you carry yourself. Taking care of yourself is one of the many things you can do to build your self-esteem. When you feel good, you look good, and you do great things.

Understanding the Power of Positivity

Understanding how to be more confident and hold higher self-esteem than you do has a variety of beneficial factors and can help you be more successful and lead a fulfilling life. None of this is possible without learning and being able to understand the power of positivity. Developing positivity can be difficult for most people because we are always trying to control our environments or overthink in many situations. Some people have low self-esteem, and it's hard to think positive when they feel so low about themselves. Another reason why positive thinking can be difficult to obtain is that we expect something to happen and often get disappointed by the outcomes if it wasn't what we expected. This sets our mind backward and forces us to think negatively about most things in our lives. However, maybe positive thinking isn't about seeing the good in everything but, in fact, accepting the bad with the good as a way of life.

So what exactly is the definition of positivity? It isn't what you are; rather, it is something you do. Scientists have been researching the power of positive thinking for a while, and they are finding that positive thinking can rewrite the trauma you have experienced. Positive thinking can help you overcome negative thinking patterns as scientists are now proving that the more you practice using a positive mind, the better at it you will become. This suggests that positive thinking is a learned skill, not something you are born with and know how to do automatically.

Positive thinking is perhaps one of the easiest things to do; however, based on an individual's experiences, their mind will automatically look for the negatives. The habit of thinking positive is more difficult than most would like to admit.

A few ways that you can implement positivity into your life are as follows:

Become Mindful and Aware

Mindfulness has been around for centuries and has been proven to develop stronger neural connections, help people be more creative, experience better memories, make better choices, and make you overall calmer. To develop mindfulness, you must learn to do the following:

1. Observe your thoughts and your surroundings. Do not label any thought or experience as good or bad. Instead, just be with them. Observe them and be nonjudgmental about them.

2. Do one thing at a time instead of trying to multitask. For example, if you are having a conversation, only have the

conversation. Listen effectively without responding right away. Give yourself time to think, then respond effectively. Put your phone and any other distractions away, and just focus on one thing.

3. Be alone with yourself for at least five to ten minutes every day. This is the time when you do absolutely nothing and just observe and be mindful of what is happening inside you and around you. This means no phone, no books, no TV, no music—just you and your thoughts.

Be Grateful

Most people have such busy lives that they forget about the small things that got them to where they are. Pay attention to the small and big things that you are grateful for. Here are some examples of what to be thankful for:

1. You woke up today.

2. You have a family to love and care for.

3. You got to drink a nice warm cup of tea.

4. You have hot water to take a shower.

5. You have things to look forward to.

Start Small

As positivity is something you do and learn rather than something you are born with (you are not), you must start small. This happens when you become aware so that you can catch the positive moments that happen in your life. Did someone make dinner today? Did you mess up at work and felt negative about it? Use these opportunities to be positive. Gradually and over time, you will start to see more positivity and then obtain it automatically.

Change Your Environment

Sometimes negativity is all around us—in our workplace, our home, our relationships, etc. Although it is important to look for positivity in your life, you should also know how to change your surroundings when negativity becomes overwhelming. Here are a few things you can do to change your negative environment to a positive one.

1. Hang out with positive people and those who support you and your beliefs.

2. Try new things, like joining a book club or volunteering at your nearest foodbank.

3. Read inspiring and motivating articles on the Internet.

4. Have sticky notes everywhere of positive sayings and

affirmations.

5. Have a positive buddy. For example, if your friend is trying to be more positive, call them every day at the end of the day and talk about all the positive things you accomplished or thought about today.

Journal

Journaling is one of the most beneficial things you can do if you are going through a challenging time and find it difficult to be positive. Journaling allows you to write out what your stresses are, then take a look at what you wrote from a third-person perspective. Through journaling, you will be able to see the positives through the negatives because the thoughts are now put down on paper rather than floating around in your head. Some people have journals strictly for stress and negative thoughts. Others have organization and planning journals. And a few others have positivity journals. Find out which type of journaling is most beneficial to you and make that a habit every day.

By taking small steps toward positivity each day, you can rebalance your life and rewire your brain to look on the brighter side of everything. Being positive isn't about staying happy and fulfilled; it's more about learning how to be positive through tough times and being with the negative if you cannot control something.

Chapter Overview

Understanding yourself is about knowing who you are as a person, what you stand for, and what you value most. From understanding more about yourself, you can then start learning how to be self-confident in who you are as a person. From that, self-esteem becomes naturally balanced into your life without you making much of an effort. If this sounds about right, there is only one more step to follow while getting to know yourself, and that's about implementing positivity into your life. As you can see, you cannot have one without the other as self-esteem, self-understanding, self-confidence, and positivity are all connected one way or another. In the next chapter, you will learn all about self-care and how to understand the benefits of self-worth, self-respect, self-love, and self-talk.

Chapter 2: Personality and Self-Worth

Self-worth is defined as a person sensing their own value or worth as an individual. There are multiple ways a person can value themselves and assess their worth as an individual. Although in some sense self-worth is the same as self-esteem, the two are actually quite different from each other. Self-worth is more about valuing your internal beliefs and morals as a person and less about measuring yourself based on your actions. In short, self-worth is about who you are, not what you do, while self-esteem is based on what you do. In other words, self-esteem, in this sense, is quite the opposite. However, self-esteem and self-worth share many similarities. High self-esteem focuses on comparing oneself to others, but self-worth solely relies on how a person sees themselves without anyone else's opinion, which, in another sense, shows high levels of self-confidence.

The first step in developing or improving your self-worth is to stop comparing yourself to others and setting high expectations of yourself. The one thing that stands in the way of improving your self-worth is your inner critical voice. Your inner critic plays a large part in how you think. When you think negatively, your critical inner voice gets in the way. Thinking positive can trump or control those pesky negative thoughts. Understanding ourselves on a deeper level and fully getting to know ourselves is the first step in overcoming those destructive voices in our heads that tell us we can't do anything. We have to foster self-worth and practice self-compassion. Being kind to ourselves is the next step to feeling worthy. Below are the three steps to practicing self-compassion:

1. Acknowledge and observe your suffering and pain.

2. Be kind to yourself and caring for your own suffering.

3. Remember that imperfection and mistakes happen to all of us, and these things need to happen in order for personal growth.

Helping others and being kind to people will give you an extreme mental and physical boost of self-worth. So volunteer when you can or give the homeless a sandwich. Overall, by being kind to yourself through healthy habits and mental exercises, you can control or cope with your internal critic, thus building self-worth. Do new things and enjoy activities that are beneficial to your personal beliefs. In doing so, you will develop and grow your own self-worth.

What Is Self-Love?

Self-love is when you know when and how to take care of yourself because you know within self-worth that you deserve to be taken care of. Who better to take care of you than you? Some people may think that self-love means you develop narcissistic traits or become overly selfish in getting what you want and need. In fact, this very much the opposite. Self-love means that you have accepted your weaknesses and appreciate all that you are. In other words, it's the ability to love yourself through your faults and your shortcomings. So how does one take care of themselves and accept all their own faults? Through self-compassion. The way to do this is to look at yourself as though you would a friend or someone you love, and then ask yourself how you would treat them. Whatever that answer is, that is exactly how you should treat yourself. To love yourself is to give yourself what your brain, body, and soul need so that you nourish and grow into the person you want to be.

Some people think that buying new clothes or reading inspirational quotes or even getting involved with someone who makes you feel good is giving yourself love. It's not. These are only temporary fixes, and they do not benefit you in the long run if your goal is to love yourself more. Here is why. Having new clothes gives us a sense of accomplishment (especially if we have worked hard for them) but not love. Reading inspirational articles gives us a sense of satisfaction, but only for a short amount of time. Getting involved in a relationship that makes us feel good and loved is how we obtain love from other people. However, the honeymoon stage will fade, and then the tough part of the relationship happens. If you don't learn to love yourself, then arguments and disagreements will be more challenging to manage. Self-love is more than just making yourself feel good through materialistic things or self-accomplishment. It's about fully appreciating yourself through actions that support and develop your intellectual, spiritual, and physical growth.

Here are a few things you can do to practice self-love:

1. *Be mindful.* Just like practicing mindfulness for positivity, you can also practice mindfulness when trying to develop self-love. You can practice being mindful for just about anything. However, when you start your meditation or awareness strategies for observance, make sure you know what your intent is, which will help you get closer to your end goal. To get long-term relaxation and awareness motivation, you must learn to practice mindfulness every day and be dedicated to it before you start seeing real effects.

2. *Figure out what you need, and ignore what you want.* Loving yourself consists of giving yourself what you need rather than giving in to your wants. Most of the time, our wants are unhealthy for us. For example, if what we want is to binge-drink and party for a few days because we feel better when we do it, we are actually damaging our bodies. Or if you have an addiction to shopping and you go to the dollar store or a clothing store and end up spending money on things you don't need, you are actually training your brain that urges are more important than other important things, like food and savings. Now instead of drinking for a few days, you could have time to yourself, like taking a long bath, listening to relaxing music, or doing something for yourself that you haven't done in a while. With the money you spend on clothes that end up getting lost or given away, you could save for a nice new house or build your credit so that you can have financial security.

3. *Take care of yourself.* People who take care of themselves know what they need. They know that short-term "exciting" activities will only end up making them feel guilty or bad in the long run. This is the time to nourish yourself with healthy activities, such as exercise, eating right, proper sleep, and trusting relationships.

4. *Set boundaries.* Self-discipline and doing what you need to do for you will also build self-love. When you show high performance at work, say no to drama, do not engage in unhealthy relationships, and deplete harmful activities, you are teaching yourself boundaries. By setting boundaries, self-love comes naturally, and you will learn how to respect yourself more.

5. *Forgive yourself.* Every person makes mistakes. We sometimes delve into bad choices that we know aren't going to turn out right. We set expectations for ourselves that are too high, and we punish ourselves when we aren't perfect. Sometimes we blame ourselves when things go wrong even when we know it's not our fault. To defeat this pattern, you need to forgive yourself and be patient with who you are. Learn to accept your faults, work on your weaknesses, but most of all, enjoy the person that you are because you deserve that.

Work on one of these at a time, and eventually, you will make it through the whole list. This is not a complete list of how to love yourself, but it is a start and a point in the right direction.

What Is Self-Respect?

Most people that do not have self-respect are looking to please everyone, and usually, they have a hard time saying no. Having respect for yourself means that you know deep down that you are worthy of being treated fairly and with respect. If you are someone who seems to attract the type of people who mistreat you or if you seem to be attracted to narcissists, then you probably don't have much respect for yourself, and oftentimes, you may not even realize that you lack self-respect. However, if you don't learn how to respect yourself now, then you are more than likely going to follow the same patterns, settling for less and struggling to find your voice. You are likely to make too many commitments and let other people walk all over you. Having self-respect ensures that boundaries are solidly in place so that you are treated well and fairly in all aspects. You have to ensure that your needs and desires are met and your voice is heard.

It helps to understand what it takes to have self-respect so that you can try to develop the trait for your own personal growth. Below are some characteristics of people who have self-respect:

- being assertive

- having no toleration for people who mistreat them or talk

down to them

- not associating with unreliable people who walk all over them

- having strong boundaries in place for the people who try to take advantage of them and suck their energy

- being able to say no to unreasonable requests and not feeling guilty or pressured to say yes because they know what is good and what is unhealthy

- having clear values and boundaries in a relationship, such as no lying

- knowing the worth of their work

- no settling for less than they deserve in any situation

Do you see a pattern? Living your life with the utmost respect for yourself shows that you are dedicated and confident in every aspect of your life, which is healthy and needed. There are many advantages of having self-respect and confidence and knowing what you deserve. Some of them are as follows:

- You value and honor your desires and needs.

- You have more energy to do things for yourself and strive toward your ambitions.

- You feel equal to others, not above nor below.

- You have better friends and longer-lasting relationships.

- You respect your performance and quality in work.

- You feel a sense of fulfillment in life.

- You feel confident and worthy.

- You have a deeper understanding of trust for yourself and others.

- You follow your intuitions more.

This is not a full list of the advantages of having self-respect; however, having self-respect means that you are giving yourself permission to follow your desires and accomplish your long-term goals. This is because you know what you want, and you are dedicated to getting what you feel you deserve.

What Is a Self-Critic?

A self-critic is a person who has uncontrollable and sometimes intrusive thoughts about everything they do. You can describe a self-critic as an overthinker or someone whose brain is on automatic negative thinking pattern. Even when you try to be positive, your inner critic may say things like "You will never get the job" or "Why can't you do anything right?" The pattern of the inner critic is the nagging "voices" or thoughts that make up an internalized dialogue of negativity and self-doubt. The critical voice is the voice that criticizes our every move. It affects almost every aspect of our lives, forcing us to feel powerless and less confident in ourselves. Negative thoughts hold more power over us than we think. It can implement self-doubt, foster distrust, bring upon self-denial, account for addictions and substance use, and worst of all, promote mental illness.

For most people, the reason why negative thinking or the voice of the inner critic is so powerful is that it stems from past experiences. Before someone realizes it, the thought pattern is already developed in the brain, which is why so many of us become stressed out so easily. Some people don't realize their inner critic is taking such a huge effect on their lives, and so in order to conquer your inner critic, you must be aware when it happens. Once you are aware and can identify exactly what the negative thought says, you can start challenging it by really thinking about the thought as a whole. You can consciously take the necessary steps to let the thought intentionally go. Take control of yourself by purposely replacing the negative thought with a positive one. The trick is not to push your thoughts away but to be with them. Observe them, and then let them disappear on their own while paying no attention to them or labeling them. This strategy is called being mindful.

Once you are completely aware of your inner critic's voice, you can start to find your triggers. Triggers are when you have done something to cause your internal negativity to activate. Once you spot your triggers, the next thing to do is to reframe your state of mind upon your triggers. For example, you go to a certain friend's house, and at first, you think about how excited you are to see them. However, when you leave, you begin to ask yourself why you went there. Why do you keep this friend in your life when the reality is that they don't need you? They are only nice to you because they feel sorry for you. If it only happens with this one friend, you have to reframe your mind to find out exactly why you keep this friend around. Figure out their true intentions. Spend more time with them to prove to your brain that there is no harm in having this person in your life. If they turn out to be ungenuine, then you have just practiced self-respect and self-love. If they turn out to be really great, then you have just accomplished reframing your inner critic. The trick is not to avoid your triggers in fear of your thoughts but to dive deeper into your triggers so that they don't become a trigger anymore.

Here are just a few simple steps in order to conquer the inner critic:

1. *Identify the inner voice.* What is your thought? What is your inner critic telling you? What is the best and worst scenario? Are you fearful of something happening? Once you identify your inner critical voice, you can start to ask it questions. Be curious about why you are experiencing these thoughts. This is a challenging process wherein you learn how to identify where the thought comes from. Take a step back and view your inner critic as if it were someone telling you these things rather than yourself. Use your wise mind to combat them.

2. *Separate from the inner critic.* The next step is to write your thoughts down, or you may also record them on your phone. The details should include everything that happened at that moment. What did you do before the critic attacked? What were you thinking before negative thoughts took over your mind? What were the exact self-critical words that were said? When you do this, you can take a step back and see the thoughts in a different light or from a different perspective.

3. *Respond to your inner critic.* After writing your thoughts down or recording your situation and environment, you can then have a more realistic evaluation of yourself. For example, if your inner critic says, "I can't get anything right. I will never achieve my goals," respond to it with "It is normal to make mistakes, and as I am a human, I will struggle, but I am smart enough to know that I can accomplish my goals if I so choose." This exercise can reframe your mind and help you start to look at things differently so that in time, your automatic response to failure will be a more compassionate approach. This is showing yourself love and worthiness.

4. *Do not act on your inner critic.* You know what you want. You know your values. You know what you deserve. That is why settling for anything less would damage your esteem. Your inner critic should never get a say in how you act or what you feel as one thing is for sure—the inner critic is just in your head. When you think about this way, you can choose to let negative thoughts control you, or you can choose to fulfill your own destiny. Treat your inner critic as a bad friend who doesn't support you and doesn't want the best for you. Acknowledge your negative thoughts, but do not feed into them.

If you follow these four steps of conquering the inner critic, it will become weaker and more distant, and you will become stronger. If you take the necessary steps to free yourself from your inner critic, you will have the freedom to pursue your goals, and you will become more compassionate and considerate of yourself. When the inner critic is just a distant memory, that is when you can finally step outside the hold it has taken, and you can become a more confident individual that you deserve to be.

Chapter Overview

Self-worth revolves around self-esteem; however, the main difference is that self-worth is more about what and how you think rather than what you do in competition to someone else. Self-worth shows that one can stick to their own beliefs without the approval of someone else because that is how confident and assured they are in their own values and judgments. The inner critic can get in the way of having or developing self-worth or any kind of self-respect because it is the voice that lies to us. It's the voice that tells us things we don't believe in. It is a trap that our minds want us to fall into. However, learning ways on combating the inner critic and negative self-talk can really benefit personal growth as you will have more energy to take care of yourself and develop boundaries around self-respect and self-worth. Part of knowing what you want will help you gain the confidence to get what your empowered self deserves.

Chapter 3: What Confidence Is All About

The thing about confidence is that it takes a lot of time to build and develop but only taking seconds for it to crumble. However, true confidence never really crumbles. Confidence can start in childhood, or it can be developed over time and become a part of adulthood. It has been scientifically proven that confidence is a different aura that people carry around with them. Science has proven that when someone is confident, they have high self-worth and self-respect. They are strong leaders and have the capacity to bounce back when they fall or go through tough times. Unconfident people often second-guess themselves and dwell on their weaknesses; thus, they never make a positive change or a step forward. Their expectations of themselves are too high, and they continue to bash themselves when they fail. Confidence is not about the mistakes you have made. It's not even about the many weaknesses that people have. Confidence is about knowing and believing that you are good enough. It's about going after what you want and what you are most passionate about without thinking that you are going to fail or mess up. Confident people know they aren't perfect, but they accept what they can do and let go of what they can't.

Here are a few traits that a confident person has developed or mastered:

1. *They have poise.* Walking with confidence.

2. ***They maintain eye contact.*** They always look at the person they are speaking to as they are not afraid to look someone in the eye.

3. ***They are firm in their ways.*** They have boundaries that hold their values in place, and they are strict about them. They stay true to themselves and go forward in life with their own personal beliefs.

4. ***They are not conscious of their appearance.*** Confident individuals don't care what others think of them because they believe that they look good as they take pride in their appearance.

5. ***They are self-assured.*** They have a good head on their shoulders and are willing to tackle almost anything because they are self-assured.

6. ***They do the right thing.*** Even if it can hurt themselves or someone else, a confident person always feels better by doing the right thing. They don't give in to peer pressure and know that what they feel in their heart is right. Confident people have strong intuitions.

7. ***They aren't afraid to be wrong.*** When they are wrong, they admit their mistakes, and they talk about them. They know when to apologize and when to be assertive in requesting what they need.

8. ***They do not hog the spotlight.*** Confident people are

not selfish because they don't need the attention of others to make themselves feel good. They know that they are good enough for themselves and hold true to their own thoughts and feelings. So they let someone else have the spotlight.

9. ***They aren't afraid to be embarrassed.*** Confident people will do random silly things because they aren't afraid to be funny.

10. ***They do not put others down.*** In fact, they build people up because they know right from wrong. Confident people don't like to waste their time with unnecessary drama or conflict as they know it brings their own beliefs and self-respect down.

11. ***They are assertive.*** A confident individual will not tolerate excuses or being lied to. They know when to help someone and when to walk away. Generally speaking, the confident individual will help someone who wants to be helped and knows the difference.

Although it may come easy for some people to be confident, for others, it can feel like a daunting task that is difficult to succeed at. A confident person does not have to obtain all these traits, but even having one or two of them is a good step toward confidence. Don't be afraid to be confident. Being confident is not being self-centered or narcissistic. If you are true to yourself and understand the big difference between confidence and narcissism, then you will be fine, and you are well on your way to being who you deserve to be.

Self-Esteem and Self-Confidence

Self-esteem and self-confidence have many similarities and also a variety of differences. They are both referred to as how you feel about yourself; however, self-esteem is more about how you feel about yourself overall. Self-esteem is how much self-love and positive regard you have for yourself, whereas self-confidence mainly focuses on your abilities. Someone may have high self-esteem, but they may not be very confident in certain aspects of their life, like how they are in topics such as math. When you learn how to take care of yourself, build your self-worth, define who you are, and love yourself through your faults, you are building self-esteem. High self-esteem stems from being confident in knowing that you deserve to be taken care of, that you are worthy, and that you do respect yourself. So as you increase your overall feeling of worth, you are also increasing your confidence level.

In other words, building self-confidence comes from your external experiences, whereas self-esteem comes from an internal experience. Self-esteem refers to how we feel about ourselves from the inside. It reflects the way we relate to our own sense of entitlement. Self-confidence reflects how we see ourselves in the outside world as we go through different circumstances and directions.

In order to build and develop your self-esteem, you must do the following:

- Listen to your true self (intuition).

- Challenge the inner critic.

- Be nice to yourself.

- Take care of yourself and go after what you want.

- Reward yourself often.

- Be supportive of others and patient with your learning process.

- Validate your accomplishments.

Someone can have more confidence than they have self-esteem or more self-esteem than they have confidence. With that said, if we have more self-esteem and less confidence, we will end up being more resilient when we fail. This is because our image of yourself comes before our confidence at a higher level, therefore acting as a foundation for when we mess up. If we hold a higher confidence level but less self-esteem, we may not feel very good about our accomplishments due to the constant negative chatter inside our brains. As you can see, having low self-esteem is actually more damaging than having confidence. However, if you work on your self-esteem, you are also working on boosting your confidence level. By doing the things listed above, you can help yourself to obtain a higher level of self-esteem in which confidence will come naturally and automatically for you.

How Negative Thoughts Affect Our Behavior

When you are asleep, your subconscious mind takes over, and when you wake up, the thoughts from your subconscious mind enter your conscious mind. Some of these thoughts include "Wake up," "No, I am sleeping," "I'm so tired," "Time to take a shower," "I am too lazy," "That dream was funny." The subconscious thoughts that we have are often uncontrollable, and they pop up at random times. However, we are actually in control of what happens in our subconscious minds. The more we think one way, the more it gets stuck into our subconscious. So if we choose to think positively, over time, we will wake up and think positive. If we allow our inner critic to take control, then negative thoughts will slip through the most. Our actions are the result of our subconscious minds. Our actions are based on the thoughts that creep through our minds. If you learn how to control your subconscious mind, you can actually help it to bring more positivity to your life, which will make you feel better. If you feel better, you feel more confident as well.

Three things you can do to reprogram your subconscious mind is to use positive self-talk, commit to correcting your negative thoughts, and practice a more balanced way of thinking (being rational). Every time you realize your thoughts are negative or dark, observe them. After that, replace them with a positive statement. See chapter 2 for more advice on how to let go of the inner critic. Reprogramming your subconscious mind is so important because if you let it take over, it will run your life. Everything that goes into your head will be acted out as part of your behaviors. Simply put, if you think negatively, you are putting forth negative energy into the universe, and negative things will happen. When you promote positivity, you will give out positive energy into the universe, and positive things will happen to you. The way you view life is all about how you think and perceive it. The choice is ultimately up to you, so it would be wise to sit down and make a list of all the things you want to obtain in your life. What kind of person do you want to be? Where do you want to end up? What is the most important thing to you right now? These questions can help you stay on track when it comes to thinking positive and gaining your sense of confidence.

Chapter Overview

Being positive is what being confident is about. By this, I mean that when you act with good behaviors, think with certainty, do right by others, and maintain self-worth, you can become self-confident in anything that you choose to do. Self-esteem is about how you think of yourself, and confidence is about what you do with your self-esteem. If you develop a negative perspective on life, you will find that both your confidence and self-esteem is low. If they are low, then you may find it difficult to live a fulfilling and satisfying life. The rest of this book will help you define who you are and give you useful tips on how to implement positivity and stay on a balanced level of self-esteem and confidence.

Part Two: Solution and Steps

Now that you know the importance of understanding yourself and have defined what self-esteem and confidence are, the second part of this book focuses on how you can overcome the inner critic and become a confident individual. This section of this self-esteem workbook will help you understand yourself on a deeper level. It will also help you maintain a steady, balanced structure of living the life you want. We all have choices, but most of the time, we ignore the paths we want to choose because we are so used to doing the same thing all the time. Doing the same thing keeps us in our comfort zone, while doing anything different seems scary or out of the ordinary. In chapter 6, you will learn how to overcome your fears so that you can take the next step into loving yourself. Before we get to that chapter, you first must understand how to accept yourself for who you are. You also need to understand why it's so important to change your negative state of mind. If you stick to what you know, which my guess hasn't worked for you, then you may experience some anxiety revolving the next steps in life. When we don't take chances on ourselves and we don't overcome the feeling of being stuck, we actually create more anxiety for ourselves. Humans are social creatures and need to experience new things. If we stay stuck doing the same thing, living the same loop, we get bored and then start to wonder what life is all about.

Part of growing into yourself and having the confidence to accomplish whatever goals you set for yourself is taking care of yourself so that you can feel better about yourself. Self-love is important in building your self-esteem, and in the second part of this self-help workbook, I will teach you how to stick with a steady routine so that you can feel empowered and confident. Once you have all the facts, you can then make loving yourself a habit. Wouldn't it be nice to kick the inner critic in the butt and develop a sense of worthiness? You bet it would be, so take no more time and read on.

Chapter 4: How to Overcome Your Thoughts and Accept Yourself

Self-acceptance is the key characteristic in self-love and building self-esteem. It's when you know and understand yourself on a deeper level but are okay with all of who you are. You accept your weaknesses, and you know what you are good at. Self-acceptance is about knowing that you can improve based on these strengths and weaknesses and being completely patient with yourself during the process of personal growth. If one day you look at yourself and feel as though you are disgusted or unhappy with yourself, the step to self-acceptance is to ask yourself why. Do you wish you were someone else? What is it about yourself that you don't like so much? Is it your appearance? Is it your personality? The good thing is that personalities can be changed and altered, and so can appearances. This takes a more dramatic effect. When you learn how to acknowledge your habits and behaviors and stop comparing yourself to other people, you can start to improve your life. Working toward self-growth is the most important step in learning how to accept yourself. One cannot truly accept who they are if they don't truly know who they are.

This is what self-acceptance looks like:

- loving yourself for who you are

- accepting your attitude, skills, and appearance

- being compassionate toward yourself

- not being judgmental of yourself and your failures

- being able to admit and accept your shortcomings

- accepting that your past doesn't define you and so you don't need to dwell on it

When you see your mistakes, you can learn to live with them and learn from them. Accepting your present position as it is right now is the only thing you can control, so it is your responsibility to make the most out of this moment. By seeing your mistakes and learning to live completely in the moment, you will find ways to improve in areas of your life you are not so proud of. This could be your career; perhaps you aren't doing what you love. Part of accepting yourself is acknowledging that you don't like what you do but at the same time looking for ways to do what you love later. For example, if you work as a professional cleaner but your passion is to be a mechanic, then you brainstorm ideas on how to save up the money to get to the first step of accomplishing this. Ask yourself what is standing in the way of your dream. Tackle those barriers and go for it. When you learn self-improvement strategies, you can decrease the feelings of anger and resentment toward yourself and actually do what you have wanted to do. The first step in doing what you love, being who you want to be, and branching out to better things is to change your negative state of mind. There are many techniques that foster personal growth and self-acceptance. Here are some of them:

- observing your thoughts and actions through mindfulness

- changing the way you think (that is, challenging the inner critic)

- repeating positive mantras in stressful times

Self-acceptance does not come easy to some people. This is why so many people read self-help books and take anxiety classes. When we are children, life is much easier or at least should be. Then from our childhood, we turn into adolescents. We want to spread our wings and be rebellious. In this process, we are truly trying to define who we are. We are shaping ourselves into the kind of adults that we want to be. Once we become adults, most of us have no clue what we are doing. Adulthood comes so fast. The experiences that we go through in this life shape us and our minds. This is why it may be so difficult for some of us to love ourselves and accept who we truly are right now. In the adolescent years, some experiences interfere with our confidence. Peer pressure is very strong. As adolescents, we feel as though we need to fit in or look and act a certain way to become accepted. As children, it might be that our parents didn't show the love and support we needed. Some people may develop abandonment issues or substance abuse throughout their lives. Other people may have had to grow up in foster families, so they already feel unloved and unwelcomed into the world. The experiences we go through shape us into who we are today. Self-acceptance is about acknowledging what has shaped you but not letting your past define who you want to be. It's about changing your state of mind and overcoming the myths of what people have told you, thinking that it is never too late to grow into what you deserve to be.

Ask yourself, "Who do I want to be?" Is it a confident businessman/woman? Is it a nurturing parent? Is it a creative loner? Then ask yourself, "Who am I now?" Is it a reserved friend? A selfish spouse? A broken individual? Finally, say this to yourself, "It doesn't matter who I am today, what got me here, and who I am going to become. What matters is that I am here, I am who I am, and I am proud." In reality, this is all that self-acceptance truly is—just knowing what you want, being able to define who you are, and not allowing the past to shape you. If you have the ability to wipe the slate clean and start over or if you (God forbid) get in a horrible accident that wipes your memories and you have the chance to restart your life, what would you do with it? Whatever the answer is, start from there. Keeping that in mind, here are a few tips on how to start your road to self-acceptance:

1. *Be good to yourself.* The first step in accepting yourself is that you need to let go of being so critical and judgmental of yourself. The only person who criticizes you more than anyone else is you, so practice kindness. You can practice kindness by doing the following:

- Reward yourself for big and small achievements.

- Treat yourself once a month or once every two weeks.

- Save 10 percent of your paycheck.

- Relax more.

- Become best friends with yourself and learn more about yourself.

- Implement some "me time" every day.

- Don't take on too much for you to handle.

2. Face your fears. It could be your inner critic that keeps you fearful or the mistakes that hold you back. You may have a habit of overthinking, or you may be someone who needs to control every circumstance. Facing your fears head-on will keep you moving forward rather than get you stuck. Doing what you know is easy, and doing something new is scary or unfamiliar. However, if you want to see change, you have to take baby steps toward them. Having a list of things you are afraid of along with your goals is a good place to start. Here are a few things you can do to face your fears:

- Make a list of your fears and goals.

- Make a fear ladder (explained in chapter 6).

- Write inspiring quotes to help you get past your fear.

- Change one thing every day.

- Sit with your fear for a small amount of time, then extend it gradually.

3. *Practice positivity.* Practicing positivity will help you stay on track toward your goals. In this case, your goal is to appreciate and accept yourself more. When your inner critic sneaks up on you, observe the thought and replace it with a positive affirmation. When you take a look at your environment and your group of friends, determine what can be changed, what can be fixed, and what benefits you the most. Here are a few things you can do to practice positivity:

- Have a notebook of positive quotes with you always.

- Have sticky notes around your house where you can tell yourself something good every day.

- Call up a supportive and positive friend for a positivity boost.

- Do something fun.

- Start a new hobby.

4. *You are not perfect.* No one is perfect, so why try to be? Every flaw that you have—e.g., your frizzy hair, your freckles, your insecurity about your personality—all makes up for who you are. Self-acceptance is not about what your past defines you to be; it's more about being able to look at yourself in the mirror and accept all the imperfections about yourself. So you messed up at work, or you dyed your white clothes pink. Maybe you said something out of anger or acted impulsively to your frustrations. Accept that these things happen, and while it's in the past, all you can do is leave it there. Strive to improve. If you can mend a relationship or fix a mistake, do it. If you can't, learn to accept that being imperfect is who you are. Nothing is wrong with that. Here are some things that will help you to practice accepting imperfections:

- Do not dwell on the past.

- Be patient with yourself.

- Do not dwell on conflict.

- Change what you can change, and let everything else work itself out.

- Laugh at your mistakes and make a tough situation humorous.

- Be weird and silly.

- Dance or sing horribly on purpose.

5. Believe in yourself. Most people struggle because they feel insecure about whether or not they can do something. By having this frame of mind, you actually set yourself up for failure. For example, if you are preparing yourself for a speech and you say, "I can't do this," "I am totally going to fail," "What if no one likes it?" etc., you will deliver your speech thinking you will screw it up, which will make you nervous, and you may actually screw up. On the other hand, if you go into it thinking, "I am nervous, but I totally got this," "I am going to nail it," "If I don't do well, it won't be as bad as I am making it seem," you set yourself up to overcome your fear of speeches, and you develop self-confidence, which overall boosts your self-esteem. Believe in yourself. You can do anything you set your mind. You have been through or survived worse before. Think about all the times you got up after a mistake and rocked life when it tried to bring you down. Here are some things you can do to practice believing in yourself:

- Push past the discomfort or fears and myths.

- Put yourself out there, not caring what other people think.

- Stay positive.

- Create mantras that you can. "Can't" is just the word "can" with a *T*.

- Trust yourself. Trust that no matter the outcome, every experience is an opportunity to grow.

6. *Push forward and be resilient.* When we fail, we learn what we can do and what we can do better at. It's only through our mistakes that we get to know ourselves on a deeper level, so push past the fear of rejection, ignore the inner critic, believe that you will succeed, and stand back up when you fall down. Find your passion, figure out what drives you the most, shoot toward

54

your goals, and strive to be better at what you're not good at. Doing these things can help you be more confident and over time. You will start to see that things don't always end badly, and your self-esteem will increase as well. Here are some things you can do to be more resilient:

- Always move forward.

- Be supportive of yourself.

- Be decisive and assertive.

- Create strong boundaries.

- Accept that change is part of life.

- Look for self-discovery opportunities.

- Do what you are good at, and improve what you aren't.

If you are not accepting of yourself, you must change that mindset. As hard as this can be, changing your mindset is perhaps the most beneficial things you can do when it comes to personal growth. When you develop an understanding of yourself, you will start to discover ways that you learn best. What makes you feel good? What helps you strive forward? Is there someone who can help you? These are important questions to answer for your own personal understanding of what accepting who you are is all about. Anything and everything that you do (whether it's developing a new hobby or learning a new skill) takes time. When you dedicate yourself to accepting who you are, you are teaching your brain how to discipline yourself, which will set your mind up to do other things like thinking positively, being confident, and taking care of yourself. A skill is something you must learn. Learn to be patient with yourself and stay motivated because you deserve to feel confident and worthy.

Changing Your State of Mind

Part of knowing who you are is not only understanding the good but knowing what holds you back from your full potential. Accepting your faults and improving your weaknesses are just a small part of learning what you can accomplish when it comes to personal growth and self-esteem. A big part that holds most of us back from working on ourselves is our mindset. Negative and unhelpful state of mind is the cause of most of our problems. Negative thinking holds us back. Our inner critic will stop us from moving forward. Do not believe too much of what it tells us. One thing is certain—if you feel miserable and lonely, your mind is the one that develops that feeling. If you want to be positive and successful, you need a mindset that supports your efforts. Oftentimes, we turn to others for validation, and we don't get it. What you should be doing is to look inward at yourself for the reassurance and validation that you crave. It's time to wipe away the infectious negative state of mind and experience a world where you aren't second-guessing, worrying, overthinking, and being vulnerable to your insecurities. Here is a list of the negative thinking patterns that keep you feeling insecure and a lack of self-love:

1. *Scarcity*. This is the belief that there isn't enough and that you aren't enough. There isn't enough money, possibilities, opportunities, resources, etc. The truth of the matter is that what you think to be true will always be true. So if you feel as though there isn't enough, then the resources and things won't ever be enough. Program your mind to think that there is enough, and there will be.

2. *Other*. This is the belief that something or someone else is the root of all your problems. It's the belief that you are never wrong, so you point the blame elsewhere. Your challenges, your misfortune, and your problems are never the cause of someone else. You are always in charge of your choices. Your decisions define the outcome in which you can learn from. Having the belief that others are responsible for your misfortunes is to have the belief that you lack the power to change or choose. The truth is that no one person or situation has the power to change your outlook or your mistakes; it's you and you alone that has this power.

3. *Imposter*. Imposter syndrome stems from a lack of confidence. This is the belief that other people may discover that you are not who you appear to be. This belief will kill your dreams and deprive you of the gifts that you have yet to discover. Be who you want to be, and trust that anyone else who sees less than you believe you are doesn't know you well enough to make that judgment.

4. *Cynicism.* This way of thinking makes a person believe that you cannot trust or put your faith into anyone. When you are skeptical of the intentions of others, then you are allowing yourself to sit by and try to deal with everything all on your own. While independence is a positive trait, not putting your trust into someone else may be the one thing standing in the way of your success.

5. *Ungrateful.* The lack of gratitude suggests that you are unappreciative of what you have because you're always looking for more. Even when you do get more, you lack the gratitude to believe that what you have is good enough. It's okay to strive for more; however, being appreciative of the things you have now is an attractive quality in anyone, and it shows great confidence.

6. *Entitlement.* This type of belief revolves around the thought that you are entitled to have or obtain whatever you want without suffering consequences or working for something. It's the thought that life will hand you things because you are special and above everyone else. When you think this way, it's like you are waiting around for someone to recognize that you are deserving of something—in most cases, it never comes. Feeling this way can develop a sense of unworthiness and make you resent yourself and others around you. Reverse this belief by doing things for others without the expectation of getting noticed. Reward yourself for the things you feel are deserving rather than waiting on someone else.

7. *Nihilism.* Is there no meaning in your life? Do you feel as though you are spinning in circles with no purpose or direction? This is called nihilism. It is the belief that there is no meaning or purpose in your life. Success is about discovering your true passion and purpose. Everyone is good at something, but they do something else because it's what they know and what is familiar to them. Find something worth fighting for, and fight for it. This is how you will find true meaning.

These ways of thinking are infectious and can take over how you view your world and everything that's in it. Pessimism is the root of these infectious thought patterns, and implementing positivity into your life will reverse the effects these beliefs have on you. Be aware of these thought patterns and beliefs, then replace them with positive ones. Overcome them with a better sense of beliefs.

Chapter Overview

The fact of the matter is that you must first learn to understand yourself fully before you can accept yourself and all your faults that come with your personality. In this process, you need to be aware of how your inner critic traps you into believing you are less than. One thing that is for sure when it comes to overcoming the inner critic is that *you are what you allow yourself to be.*

Your world revolves around the way you perceive things and the way you choose to think. If you choose to think negatively, all you are going to see are negatives, and you will have a negative self-image. If you choose positivity, then you can develop positivity in the way you see things, and there will be opportunities for growth. In this chapter, you learned the negative beliefs your mind traps you in and how to overcome them. You also learned that self-acceptance is the first step that you need to take toward building self-esteem and confidence. In the next chapter, you will learn about anxiety and how anxiety and fear can turn into an anxiety disorder. You will also learn why it's important to stop your unhealthy habits now.

Chapter 5: Why Anxiety Happens

What Is Anxiety?

Some people define "anxiety" as a sense of uncomfortable feelings. Others define it as a state of mind that involves fear. Fear is a part of our response to anxiety; however, fear and anxiety are a bit different. Fear tells us that you are in actual danger, and you are right to feel that danger is present. Anxiety, on the other hand, revolves around unpleasant feelings. There is a sense of uneasiness, even when there is no danger present. Anxiety gives you a heightened feeling that something bad is going to happen—e.g., the *possibility* of someone jumping out and scaring you. Anxiety reacts to our intuition or instinctive nature about things. This happens when we meet someone for the first time and something doesn't feel right. Another example is when we walk down a dark alley alone and our senses become heightened as if we were on our guard. Anxiety is normal and beneficial to have sometimes. It is the body's natural response to stress. However, anxiety can become dangerous if you were to develop an anxiety disorder. This is when anxiety controls your mind and your body through anxiety attacks to the point that it disrupts many aspects of your life, and it can last longer than six months.

What Are Anxiety Disorders?

By definition, an anxiety disorder is when you feel intense fear almost all of the time, which can make it very difficult to relax. In extreme cases, anxiety can turn into agoraphobia (not able to leave your home) or depression (feelings of extreme sadness 90 percent of the time). An anxiety disorder may stop you from being social. It can cause you to avoid things like riding the elevator or talking on the phone. There are eight different types of anxiety disorders, each with similar symptoms:

1. **Panic disorder:** You feel a sense of impending doom that results in panic attacks randomly for no given reason. This can result in someone fearing another panic attack, which can make the panic disorder worse.

2. **Phobia:** There is an overwhelming fear of a certain person, place, thing, activity, or situation.

3. **Social anxiety:** This is a disorder that revolves around the fear of others, how other people think of you, how they could be judging you. You fear that people are out to get you.

4. **Obsessive-compulsive disorder (OCD):** There are consistent irrational negative thoughts that result in a person acting out their impulses and repeating certain behaviors based on their OCD.

5. **Separation anxiety:** This is an overwhelming fear of being away from home (stems from agoraphobia) or loved ones.

6. **Agoraphobia:** This is the fear of not being able to escape a situation or place and being trapped, so a person isolates themselves from the outside world.

7. **Health anxiety:** This is also known as hypochondria. It is intense anxiety about your health. When a little symptom arises, the person automatically fears they are unhealthy.

8. **Post-traumatic stress disorder (PTSD):** This happens when a person has recurring memories and panic attacks associated with a traumatic event.

Each of the eight anxiety disorders has its own characteristics and symptoms, but all of them represent the same initial symptoms during an anxiety attack. When someone experiences an anxiety attack, they feel an instant rush of stress, worry, and fear. Anxiety attacks can come out of nowhere, or it can be brought on by someone's thoughts or their environment.

The following are signs of an anxiety attack:

- feeling as though you are going to pass out

- dry mouth

- sweating or overheated

- restlessness

- distress

- fear

- numbness and tingling

- increase in heart rate

- shortness of breath (as though you can't breathe) or a choking feeling

Panic attacks are scarier than anxiety attacks, and although they share some similar symptoms, they are not the same. Below is a list of symptoms of a panic attack:

- a heavy and pounding heartbeat

- an abnormally fast heart rate

- hyperventilation

- sudden headache

- excessive and uncontrollable shaking

- nausea

- chest pain (as if an elephant is standing on your chest)

- feeling out of your body (derealization)

Panic attacks usually come on suddenly with no apparent reason, and they are very scary to the individual experiencing it. Someone may feel as though they are having a heart attack or are going to die. They have an overwhelming sense of impending doom.

Anxiety disorders take a large effect on your brain and your body. However, the good news is that with the right treatment (consultation with a doctor or professional), dedication, and mindset, you can overcome or decrease feelings of anxiety. People who experience severe anxiety and an abnormal number of panic and anxiety attacks may need to see a clinical counselor, alongside taking prescription drugs that are prescribed by a psychiatrist. Other times, we can mostly get away with our short-term symptoms through natural herbs, supplements, and vitamins. As long as someone can dedicate to eating healthier, getting enough exercise (both the mind and body), having a good night's rest, and avoiding substances like drugs and alcohol or caffeine, they can get better.

How Anxiety Affects the Brain

Anxiety often gets worse when someone has low self-esteem and not a lot of confidence. It's when someone doesn't know how or forgets to love themselves through self-care that feelings of anxiety and development of an anxiety disorder becomes too much to handle. But what actually happens in the brain that makes anxiety symptoms worse and the individual spiral out of control?

Typically speaking, anxiety stems from an imbalance between the emotional and thinking parts of the brain. In short, the prefrontal cortex or limbic system activates the amygdala, which is responsible for reacting to sudden threats and danger. This is essential in threatening situations. However, in nonthreatening situations, the amygdala is responsible for sending signals to other parts of the brain to activate the fight-or-flight response.

The fight-or-flight response happens when a chemical called cortisol gets released, sending adrenaline throughout the body. Cortisol and adrenaline work together, and they are responsible for making someone see longer distances, run faster, talk and think faster, and become stronger. It's the preparation to help someone get out of a dangerous situation. If there is no sudden danger or anything threatening going on, a person's panic attack is the result of the aftermath of the adrenaline. It leaves someone with tingling extremities and uncontrollable breathing patterns.

Another part of the brain that gives false alarms or too much anxiety is the hippocampus, which is responsible for memory function. Everything that we see and experience is what the hippocampus takes in. It then sends these memories to other parts of the brain to be stored and filed. The problem with anxiety and the hippocampus is that the hippocampus limits most memories except for traumatic ones or anything that is associated with anxiety and stress. In other words, memories revolving around failure, threat, and danger are filed deep within the hippocampus. These memories then become triggered in the future.

Good memories revolving around safety, certainty, and stability get pushed aside. They are stored differently to make room for the traumatic ones. With that being said, if someone does not seek professional help for their anxiety and low self-esteem issues, they will find themselves in a never-ending loop of anxiety and stress, which can shrink and change the form of the hippocampus. This type of damage to the hippocampus can result in more painful memories, bringing on flashbacks, excessive triggers over what seems to be nothing, and an overload of false signals resulting in out-of-the-blue panic attacks.

Benefits of the Need to Change Your State of Mind

One of the first and best ways to overcome anxiety is to change your state of mind. Change the way you see yourself and build confidence through working on your self-esteem and independence. Learning how to balance your mind and bring your focus to what's important to you can greatly affect how you choose to respond to difficult situations. When we damage our hippocampus and amygdala, we may find it extremely difficult to relax and release our stress. This results in stress and anxiety taking over, as mentioned. To reverse these effects, you should make it a point to learn more about yourself by changing your mindset and purposely changing how you react to complicated situations.

Listed below are the benefits of learning how to change your mindset:

1. *Mindfulness becomes easier.* When you first start meditating and being aware of your surroundings and what is happening in your body, you may make a few mistakes or become easily distracted. With practice, mindfulness can help you unwind, relax, and change the way you see things. At the beginning of your practice, you will have to bring all your focus to your breath. Over time, as you get better at mindfulness meditation, you can work on retraining your brain by paying attention to your thoughts. The more dedicated you are in retraining your mind, the easier mindfulness will become.

2. *Enhanced immune reaction.* As much as meditation needs to be worked on then improved over time, it should only take about eight weeks to change the electrical activity in the brain. This means the effects of a damaged hippocampus and amygdala can be reversed in just eight weeks. However, it is essential not to stop after eight weeks because the benefits of meditation can positively affect your way of life. There was a study in 2003 that proved this theory. The study also researched the effects of meditation involving changing your state of mind, and it has proven that meditation can lead to an enhanced immune response. People who are capable of relaxing and unwinding their minds are less likely to get sick or catch the flu.

3. Chronic pain is reduced. We are what we think about, and we behave based on how we choose to react to things. This all happens in our minds, and we can actually change the way our bodies react to physical pain, such as joint and bone pain. Researchers have conducted a study on participants who worked on changing their state of mind. The results showed that pain, such as a little shock to the skin, was lesser in the individuals who worked on meditation to control their mindset compared to the ones who didn't.

Although not a full list of benefits, you can see how working on your brain through methods of mindfulness and meditation among other techniques can really change your state of mind, thus leading to the reversed effects of damage in the brain caused by anxiety and stress.

Things to Consider When Practicing Techniques on How to Change Your State of Mind

While you work on self-confidence and building self-esteem, you first need to remind yourself of the truths. Take the following list into consideration when practicing techniques on *how* to change your state of mind.

1. *You are not your past.* Your past experiences do not define who you are and who you choose to be. You are not defined by what someone else has said about you. Let go of this preconceived notion and breathe. Understand that you are who you want to be at this moment.

2. *You are more than what your inner critic tries to tell you.* The truth about our internal self-hatred that sets expectations that are too high and goals that we won't accomplish is that these are all just thoughts. Negative thoughts like these should never control the way we perceive the world because they are all untrue. Confidence is about being certain that the negative thoughts that arise in our minds do not control our reality. Sure, your thoughts can force you to feel bad, but like thoughts, emotions don't control who we want to be either. Your negative thoughts and emotions combined with your inventive positive attitude make up for who you want to be. Every part of you is what makes you who you are. Developing personal growth and overcoming your anxiety through these false perceptions are what allow you to strive toward being who you want to be.

3. *Other people's perceptions of you are false.* In most cases, how someone sees you is their own perception, and it is rarely ever true. An individual with high self-esteem knows that someone's opinion of them is only false projections of themselves. You may have shared your experiences and told your friends of things that have happened to you, but that doesn't mean that the way they see you is who you are. They have not walked in your shoes or lived your life. They can make opinions and give you guidance; however, only you know how you think, perceive, and feel about your given circumstances and experiences.

4. Self-worth is only how you choose to believe it. What this means is that you are worth it if you believe you are worth it. When you settle for less than that, you are teaching your brain that you deserve less. In this case, your brain will play on your emotions and thoughts and help you develop this way of thinking. When you believe that you are worth it and you choose to focus on taking better care of yourself, your thoughts will change, and so will your perception of your self-worth.

5. It's okay not to feel okay sometimes. We get in our heads most of the time because we don't give ourselves enough credit. We also believe that because we feel bad, we are bad. The truth is that when we feel bad, we don't have to ignore these feelings. We need to sit with them and deal with them patiently and nonjudgmentally. Accepting that your heart hurts or that you feel betrayed or that you are not okay is human. So be okay with not being okay.

6. You are a work in progress. Everything that you have experienced to this date has made you who you are today—the good and the bad. It does not define who you want to be, nor does it define who you are going to be. Life is about taking risks while learning how to focus your attention to what matters most. You must give yourself time to work on yourself and also reward yourself when you have made progress. Be patient and kind to yourself because you are a work in progress and you are not perfect. Being confident and self-worthy is not being perfect. We have to accept our mistakes along the way.

7. *All we have is today.* This is the last truth that you need to keep in mind. The past is done and uncontrollable, while the future is never for sure or set in stone. Focus on today. Take one step at a time. This is how you will be able to truly change the way you see yourself and reverse your anxiety.

Chapter Overview

As debilitating as anxiety can be, the best way to overcome it is by defining the truths in changing your state of mind. In chapter 7, you will learn in more detail how to change the way you see yourself while practicing self-appreciation. This is essential in your personal growth as it can reverse the effects that anxiety has on your hippocampus and amygdala so that you stop suffering from anxiety and panic attacks. In the next chapter, you will be able to define what fear is and how to deal with it to be able to see opportunities and chase after what you most desire.

Chapter 6: Dealing with Fear

Fear is the body's natural response to a perceived threat or a dangerous situation. Fear can happen before a big interview. It can happen when you are overly anxious and nervous about an upcoming event. Our minds like to play tricks on us and dream up fearful situations that don't end up turning out the way we had imagined, to begin with. So in this sense, fear can be brought on intentionally by our minds. It is how we perceive an upcoming circumstance. Fear can also come out of nowhere as you face it directly. For example, almost getting run over or into a serious accident can bring instinctive fear. Being afraid can lead you to run, freeze, hide, or do whatever you need to do to handle and cope with the perceived fearful experience.

When we are children, we fear nightmares or scary movies. As we reach adolescence, we may be scared of asking someone on a date or getting rejected. When we grow into a young adult, fear may come when we are unsure of our future. We feel afraid that we might not be able to find a job that is good enough. A person can experience fear from anything (e.g., an illness, a family member's death, an object such as a spider), or it can also stem from a mental disorder, such as social anxiety disorder.

You have two options when it comes to fear: let it control you, or let it encourage you. If you let fear control you, you may end up denying it, avoiding it, or ignoring it. However, it is still going to be there even if you are avoiding it. It's going to continue to be there until you learn ways to conquer it and move forward. For example, if a lady is not ready to have a child but finds out that she is pregnant, she can choose to ignore it, avoid it, and deny it. However, the truth is, she is only getting rounder in the middle and there is a growing baby. If you wait too long to make a decision based on what you will do, the fear will take over, and serious consequences may happen. Dealing with it head-on is the best way to go.

In this case, how would you deal with the fear of pregnancy? You would first talk to your spouse and come up with solutions around it. Are you keeping the baby? If so, how can you prepare? What can you do to make it better? In dealing with fear, no matter what form it comes in, you must figure out a course of action, then go down that path of action. If you are fearful of an object, coping with the subjective fear through exposure therapy may be the best option. This is where you would introduce yourself to the fear in small doses. For example, to overcome the fear of flying, first, you imagine yourself flying. After that, try to see a plane up close. Next, get in the plane without taking flight. And eventually, take flight when you are ready. The goal with exposure therapy is to move on to the next step only when you have conquered the previous step and have done it more than once. It's also a technique that is proven to work in people with agoraphobia.

As briefly explained in the last chapter, fear, like anxiety, creates the fight-or-flight response. This response allows us to fight harder or run faster from what we are afraid of. Instinctively, fear is what we feel when we see a big shadow, hear a low grumble in the dark, or feel a chill when we know that we are the only people in our house but sounds prove otherwise. These situations are what activates the fear response resulting in tensed muscles, goosebumps, increased heart rate, blood vessel constriction, and breathing rate quickens. These physical responses in the body can make someone seem bigger than they are. Fear enables a person to run faster due to the constrictions in the blood vessels as they dilate to carry oxygen and nutrients to the muscles faster.

Although fear forms in the same place as an anxiety trigger does (the limbic system, stemming from the amygdala and hippocampus), fear and anxiety are not the same. Fear is a short-term emotion that activates because of something. Anxiety can be long-term and will come out of nowhere, usually with more intense symptoms, such as migraines and derealization. With that being said, the amygdala works with the hippocampus and together activates the pituitary gland. The pituitary gland is where the nervous system works with the endocrine system, which is responsible for the release and intake of hormones. When we are afraid, the pituitary gland releases the adrenocorticotropic hormone into the bloodstream. When this happens, the part of the brain responsible for triggering the fight-or-flight response sends a signal to the adrenal gland, which then releases the epinephrine hormone into the bloodstream. Then cortisol is released.

All these hormones together create the rise in blood pressure and blood sugar. Your white blood cells turn fatty acids into energy so that you are able to fight harder or run faster in the face of danger. If your hippocampus, amygdala, and limbic system are damaged due to an overload of these hormone surges with no supposed threat or danger, then panic and anxiety attacks are more likely to happen out of the blue until the limbic system becomes repaired.

Fears can be internal, such as fear of failure and fear of your inner critic (fear of your own mind), or as simple and external as fear of a certain object or becoming extremely shy in social environments. When we are young, we are mainly fearless, and we face everything that scares us. Throughout our lives, we go through a series of events that shape and change us to become who we are today. If those experiences make us afraid and fearful, some regions of our brains can start to change. As instinctual as fear is, it is an emotion necessary for our survival. We feel fear as a response to activities such as bungee jumping or watching scary movies. Fear can also be brought on by something like being alone in the woods or feeling as though someone else is in your house. It is an emotion that we should respect. However, if it gets out of hand (comes out of nowhere), then we should try to overcome it.

Overcoming Shyness

Shyness results from being afraid of social situations. Sometimes a person feels shy when they have an overwhelming fear of being judged or embarrassed in front of a group of people or just one person. If the fear of social situations persists for a long period of time, it can turn into a social anxiety disorder. The symptoms of social anxiety disorder include excessive sweating, having an overwhelming fear when meeting or talking to people, and muscle tension. It is normal to feel socially anxious the first time you meet someone or if you have to get in front of a group of people. The first time you meet someone, you may feel a little cautious and afraid to open up completely and be weird—that's normal. Shyness doesn't revolve around the fear of being social; however, it represents a more reserved and standoffish attitude in social settings.

With time, effort, consistency, dedication, and commitment to change, shyness can be overcome. If your shyness is a result of social phobia or social anxiety, then help from a professional is required. In this case, if you are looking to overcome shyness from the fear of being judged in a social setting or whatever your shyness stems from, there are ways to defeat it.

1. Don't tell. More than likely, people you meet have no idea that you are shy unless you show signs of shyness. Don't be in your head if someone is judging you based on your shyness. The only people who matter right now are the ones who already know.

2. Keep conversations light. When someone else does notice or calls you out on it, keep your tone steady and casual. If it escalates into a full conversation, just remind yourself that you are who you are. Speak of your shyness lightly, and smoothly move on to a different topic if it makes you uncomfortable.

3. Change your tone of voice. If you have a habit of blushing due to your shyness, don't make blushing known as part of your shyness. Instead, see it as its own thing and say, "I have always blushed." If your shyness is a result of you fidgeting or looking off into the distance, tell yourself or the person you are speaking to that you are a normal fidgeter or that you simply listen better by looking away.

4. Avoid labeling yourself. You are who you are, and acceptance of this is all you can do. Don't label yourself as shy but simply unique in your own character.

5. Quit sabotaging yourself. Is your inner critic getting the best of you again? Ignore this internal parrot and distract your mind, or really pay attention to someone when they are talking. This will quiet your own thoughts and help you focus on the moment.

6. Know what your strengths are. It's good to do this on your own time, but make a list of all your strengths then carry it around with you. List all your positive qualities, then in a social setting where you feel anxious or nervous, read this list for a confidence booster. Let it serve as a reminder of how much you have to offer. You have the potential to be great.

7. *Choose your friends wisely.* Oftentimes we surround ourselves with people who are unhelpful, unsupportive, egotistical, or cocky. A shy person such as yourself should not pay much attention to these types of people because they will suck you dry of the things that you do feel confident about. Pay no attention to them, and surround yourself with warm, positive, and encouraging people.

8. *Be observant.* Most of the time, a shy person is observant because what they can't say makes up for what they can see. Instead of being judgmental with your observations, try to notice the people who show signs of dealing with their own insecurities. This may help you to understand that you aren't alone, which will help you overcome your shyness.

9. *Mistakes happen.* Afraid of failing or embarrassing yourself? Don't call these mistakes when they do happen because more than likely, no one noticed except for you. If they did notice, they probably aren't making a big deal out of it like your inner critic is trying to.

10. *Face your fear.* Remember that list you made? Read it now, and then face your fear head-on. Sometimes when all else fails, you just need to get out of your comfort zone and face your fear. When you do this, you may actually find that you are comfortable acting silly or loud. Sometimes you fear that you will look bad or funny in front of others, but in reality, it's just your inner critic who brings you down and makes you shy.

11. *Name your worries.* Your jitters or worries are probably the reason you feel so shy, so recognize the root cause of these, then create an action plan to eliminate them and move forward.

Shyness should not hold you back from being successful, so whether you are shy or not, use these techniques to move forward and escape your shyness.

Escaping the Fear of the Inner Critic

The inner critic is like the part of you that acts as a bully. It's the internal thoughts that get you to try to believe what it is telling you. It says things to you like "You aren't good enough," "You're such a failure," "No one likes you," "Why would you get accepted when there are other applicants?" "What makes you so special?" Do these things sound familiar? Do you blame yourself for things you can't control? Do you point out the negatives in a completely positive situation? This is your inner critic. It's the part of us where our insecurities and inner faults come to life. The inner critic wants perfection and is a fortune teller. And did you know it can actually read minds too?

The inner critic is never to be taken seriously because it is not productive, and it is never truthful, even if it seems like it's telling the truth. One thing to always remember when dealing with the inner critical part of you is that you are who you think you are. So if you listen to your inner critic telling you that you aren't good enough, then the belief that you aren't good enough becomes your reality, which then results in fear of going after opportunities and facing challenges. If you think, "I may think I am not good enough, but I know I am, and I know my own strengths and weaknesses," then you are believing against your inner critic, which can develop confidence.

Think of it this way—even though your mind may feel as though it is helping you by pointing out your weaknesses, it is actually the fear part of your brain protecting yourself from being hurt or disappointed. It is trying to stop you from being humiliated. If we listen to it, it only means we are giving in to the fear of our own minds. How do you escape this reality? Question your thoughts and ask yourself if the inner critical voice inside your head is what you would tell a close relative or a cherished friend. Probably not, and if you did, you would most likely lose this close friend resulting in loneliness. If that sounds like no fun to you, then here is what you can do to escape the fear of your inner critic.

1. Tune in. It may sound counterproductive, but when we tune into our inner critic, you can create an image of what that part of you is trying to say about you. Actually drawing it out or maybe writing it down may help, but ask yourself questions about the inner critic. How old does your voice feel? (How old were you when you first got picked on?) What does this bully look like? Does it sound like a person from your past (e.g., a parent, sibling, enemy, or ex-partner)? Does it sound familiar to someone who is in your life now? Painting a picture and getting to know your inner critic better can help you figure out the root and the trigger of it.

2. Become curious. How often does the inner critic show up? At which points in your life is it louder than normal? It may feel as though it's always there, but most likely, it is not. When you notice your inner critic talk to you, figure out what you are doing at that moment. Is it loud in social situations? Have you made a mistake that caused you imperfection? Does it demand that you stay home when you are out, or does it ask you to avoid things you enjoy? Figure out how often it comes around, and be curious about it. It may be best to keep a journal for when it does show up so that you can see the patterns and define your triggers.

3. Ask more questions. Once you have created an image of this "monster" and figured out how often it comes around, you may start to notice things about it that you never observed before. When this happens, ask it things such as the following:

- Can I help you?

- What would you like me to know?

- If I don't follow your advice, what are you afraid of that could happen to me?

- What is your reasoning behind these hurtful words?

Treat your inner critic as you would a bully. But be kind, curious, nonjudgmental, and observant.

4. Listen, then respond. Once your questions are answered, acknowledge the answers, and either ask it another question or respond to that answer. You can respond to your inner critic by reassuring it or acting on what you feel. For example, if the voice said it fears that your failure will make you even more miserable, respond with "I hear your concern, but I will not allow myself to live in fear of making mistakes" or "I won't go where I need to go in my life." Be thankful, and then move on. When you do this, you are training your brain to reverse or quiet the inner critic. You are also letting the inner critic know that it's been heard and you are controlling it rather than letting it control you.

As insane as you may feel talking to yourself, the more you respond to your inner critic, the lesser the voices will interrupt your life. Gradually, you will notice a difference in your mood and in your behavior. Try to have fun with it, and let go of the judgment as you are retraining your inner critic to calm down and be less of a nuisance.

Fear of Failure

The one truth about failure is that failure is needed to help us learn from our mistakes and grow into self-confident, self-loving individuals that we are. Failure helps us stay unique, and it is necessary for moving forward with our lives. However, when we fail, we may feel emotions resulting from our failures, such as frustration, anger, sadness, regret, shame, or embarrassed. Although these feelings are unpleasant, every emotion (whether they be negative or positive ones) serves a purpose. There are many reasons why we feel afraid to fail. These reasons are as follows:

- You may feel judged or fear being rejected if you fail.

- You are afraid of losing people because of your failures.

- You worry excessively over your failure (inner critic) in an attempt not to do it again.

- You beat yourself up over it.

- You worry about disappointing others.

The truth is that no one is perfect, and these worries brought on by the fear of failing can stop you from progressing because you hold too high of expectations for yourself. Perfectionism isn't about being perfect all the time but rather avoiding things so that you won't make mistakes. Truthfully, mistakes are bound to happen, no matter how hard you try to stop them. Acceptance of who you are, no matter what you do, creates progress and creativity about how to control your fear of failing. Once you can accept that you are going to make mistakes because you are human, you can finally start growing and changing your mindset around failure. Here are a few ways you can overcome the fear of failure.

1. *Own your fear.* When you are afraid, you can feel ashamed and regretful—ashamed because of the mistake you made and regretful because you shouldn't have done it, to begin with. However, these are false beliefs. It is not true that anything less than perfect is unacceptable. Own your fears and accept that each emotion you experience serves a purpose to you. Feeling ashamed helps you remember the event so that you don't make the same mistake again. Feeling regretful helps you to understand why you feel wrong after making a mistake. Knowing right from wrong is a positive trait to grow bonds, and it can help you through many circumstances in your life.

2. *Think before you do or say something.* The only way to avoid failing is to think about every possibility around your decision then come up with a solution. Be careful not to get too caught up in the moment as overthinking will get you nowhere. Reach out to a trusted friend or loved one and vent or explain to them your situation to gain some insight. Write down all the possibilities, and brainstorm your reasoning behind each path. Once you find a solution, don't be afraid to fail once you do it. Again, failing is a part of life that helps you to move forward in your personal growth.

3. *Be apologetic.* Say sorry to yourself and others that you have hurt. Learning to communicate the results of your failure is potentially the best way to overcome the fear of it. Accept that you aren't perfect and be okay with the fact that not everyone will get along or share the same opinion that you do. The reasons for failing was not done on purpose, and this is why they are called mistakes.

4. *Let go of control.* This step is perhaps the key to overcoming your fear of failure. By letting go of what you can't control (e.g., the future and things that have already happened), you can focus on the present moment. The only moment that matters is what you decide to do right now. Even after planning and thinking out your course of action to avoid failure, sometimes something unexpected comes up that changes everything. For example, you may have made a promise to a friend that you were going to come to their birthday. If you didn't make it due to a family emergency or the weather being horrible, you couldn't help this. Instead of seeing it as a failure, make individual plans with them to fix it.

5. *Be mindful.* Fear of failure can stem from worrying too much about the future or avoiding at all costs what happened in the past. As said in the previous step, these things are out of your control. Instead, all you can do is be completely mindful of your actions, your thoughts, and what you *can* control. Being observant works in your favor also, so you can be "mindful" of what happened and make mental notes of it. Relax and don't take everything as a big deal. Learning from your mistakes is all you can do right now.

Being fearful is okay. It helps you to stay cautious and on guard for what's to come. However, no one can predict the future—not even your inner critic. Let go of what can't be done, and be one with yourself. Try to create inner peace so that when you do fail, it won't be such a catastrophe. Understand that you are only human and you are doing the best you can. As you build your self-esteem and confidence, fear of failure will seem as though it's a thing of the past.

Chapter Overview

Being fearful, in general, causes stress and anxiety. It builds on your low self-esteem and stops you from gaining perspective or taking chances. Diving into opportunities that arise while letting go of unnecessary fear promotes confidence and growth. Part of overcoming fear is staying positive in a negative situation, getting support from trusted individuals, and staying mindful of what you can and cannot control. In this chapter, you learned that fear is instinctual and oftentimes cannot be stopped. You learned why it happens. We also discussed what happens momentarily in the brain when you feel afraid. In the next chapter, you will learn ways to appreciate yourself and find what you are most passionate about and how to love yourself fully.

Chapter 7: Awake Self-Love and Appreciation

Self-love and self-appreciation go hand in hand. Self-love is about taking care of your body, mind, and spirit to the point where you feel content and happy with yourself. Self-appreciation is the ability to appreciate all that you have, all that you have worked for, and all that you are as an individual. Appreciating who you are means that you accept who you are and you build upon your already planted foundation. Self-esteem is about learning to feel special, accept uniqueness, and be an above-average individual. However, self-appreciation just allows you to accept all that you are. Self-appreciation is not defined as accomplishing something or finding your deep desires. It's just acceptance and appreciation of why you are the way you are today.

Some people think that it is selfish to develop confidence, have high self-esteem, and respect yourself; it is not. There is a big difference between selfishness and being self-centered. Self-centered is where you are all about yourself and your needs while dismissing the needs and wants of others because it's all about you. Being selfish means that while you still pay attention to others, your main goal is to put yourself first. You can't help someone in need if you are the one who needs to be helped. You also cannot maintain promises if you already have so much on your plate. The purpose of this book is to show you that you are deserving and worthy of working on yourself and striving toward personal growth *first*. Appreciation is one of the aspects of confidence and self-esteem. It helps you value who you are and what you do. It means that you can trust your intuition, accept your strengths and weaknesses, and be at peace with your own company.

1. Honor who you are. Everyone is unique in their own way, and all too often, we look toward others for what we want because we cannot accept who we are. The media doesn't help with the newsletters and magazines all advertising ways to lose weight or technique to spice up your love life. We continuously buy into what we *should* be, how we *should* act, and why we aren't good enough. But true self-appreciation stems from when you can honor yourself completely. Come to terms with the most human part of yourself, including your ideas, thoughts, belongings, relationships, emotions, and self-image. Learning to honor all the things that make you who you are will help you see life from a different perspective so that you can build on top of the personal foundation you already possess.

2. Spend time with yourself. If you spend some alone time with yourself, you can get to know yourself better. You will understand what makes you fearful, why you feel resistant to change, and what makes you feel as though you aren't good enough to feel worthy. Self-compassion is the ability to be friendly and kind to yourself. In order to be self-compassionate, you must deal with your inner critic so that you can listen to your true self (what's underneath the self-critic). Self-acceptance can be followed in these easy ways:

- *Listen to your internal voice.* After all the chatter from the negative parrot, finding your true voice and listening to it will help you find the answers to who you really are. By tuning into your inner voice, you will understand what's most important to you, find what makes you motivated, and figure out who you truly are and what you truly desire.

- *Practice positive self-talk.* This takes two minutes in the morning, throughout your day, or before you rest at night. Positive self-talk, even if you don't believe it, can really help you get past your insecurities. Essentially, you are training your brain and fixing the damage to the limbic system by telling yourself that you can do this. Believe that you are worthy, you are deserving, you are respected, you are kind, you are unique, etc.

- *Imagine your inner child.* Life was so much simpler when we were children. We learned boundaries, control, and strength. Going back to the perception of how you view the world as a child can help you appreciate the small things, and you will be more grateful for what you have right now. Self-appreciation involves you dropping the perfectionist lens and choosing a more compassionate way instead.

- *Listen to the stories you tell yourself.* We always put labels on ourselves, such as "I for sure have anxiety," "I am a victim," "I will not succeed," "I am a failure," etc. Self-appreciation is the root of our narrative of what we decide to believe about ourselves. So when we tell ourselves that we are the victim, we start to feel victimized, and we become the victim without even trying. Reflect on your narrative. Tell your story how it is instead of exaggerating the negative or exceeding the positive.

3. Say thank you to yourself. Rather than blaming yourself for failures or other people's misfortunes, say thank you to yourself for the things you take for granted. Self-appreciation is about being thankful for a healthy body and mind, being thankful for your given talents and natural gifts, and being thankful for your weaknesses. You cannot develop internal strength without first understanding your weaknesses. These things are what we take for granted. The main difference between self-esteem and self-appreciation is that self-esteem is a personal evaluation of your self-worth. Basically, it's judging whether or not you feel as though you deserve respect and admiration. Self-appreciation is not about judging yourself based on what you feel you deserve; it's more about just accepting yourself for how you are and being grateful for what you have and what's been given to you. So how exactly do you appreciate yourself?

4. Don't wait or procrastinate. Self-appreciation requires you to just do it. Don't wait for an accomplishment or a goal to be met. Don't look for or wait for others to appreciate you. Do it all on your own because you can. Look toward what you have and don't focus on what you don't have or what you want to gain more of. These things you have should never be materialistic. Start by just being grateful for all your limbs to work properly, and then move into your internal organs. Be thankful that you have life and that your life is this way because you chose it.

5. *Use a compassionate language.* If your inner critic always pipes up with everything you do wrong, change it by replacing the negativity with kind words. Change how you talk to yourself by saying to yourself what you would say to someone you loved. For example, if you are forgetful and you forgot to do something, be accepting that you forgot. Rather than being hard on yourself, think of all the times when you weren't forgetful, and move on from this experience.

6. *Give a gift to yourself.* Do you work too hard and never appreciate yourself for working so hard? Reward yourself or treat yourself with a gift every so often to remind yourself that you are strong and are deserving of your hard work and efforts. This gift can be materialistic, such as a favorite treat, a new phone, or a video game. It can also be that you give yourself a work break. Get a massage or spend time in nature, doing one thing you enjoy the most. As long as the intention behind your gift isn't that you *want* something but that you are giving a gift out of *appreciation of yourself*, you can further develop self-appreciation.

7. *Be yourself.* Just be you. Don't try to measure up to anyone's expectations or be overly perfect in everything you do. Don't shy away from your humor and silliness for fear of being judged. Don't do something you normally wouldn't just to impress someone else. Just be yourself. Self-appreciation is developed at its strongest point when you learn to let go of the small stuff and be who you are as an individual. If you are an introvert, be an introvert. If you feel comfortable being the life of the party, then do that. Don't apologize for who you are but simply appreciate that you are who you are.

People who strive too hard to impress others never truly figure out who they are. Instead, they fall into the media trap trying to shape themselves to what they think others want them to be. Self-appreciation is about learning what truly drives and motivates you to succeed. What are your passions? What are your goals and desires? What makes you who you are and what helps you to feel at best with yourself? Answering these questions through your actions will help you develop self-appreciation.

Awake Your Self-Love

In chapter 2, we explained what self-love was and why it's essential to build self-esteem and self-confidence. No matter the original definition and how I explained it, self-love has a different meaning for everyone as it is perceived differently for each individual. Everyone has their own ways of showing that they love someone, so the definition of "self-love" is based on how someone shows love to themselves. The question is, *how* do you love yourself?

1. Put aside some time for self-love. To do this properly, you must turn off all distractions and pamper yourself. You can moisturize your feet by rubbing lotion onto them and massaging them until they feel better. Take a long bath with essential oils and bath salts to really pamper yourself through scent, feeling, and mind. Make yourself a gourmet meal. Whatever pampering yourself looks like, do it with no distractions.

2. Do something that makes you feel good. This could be something you are good at or something new you are just learning how to do. Taking a nature walk with your friends, making a road trip with your dog, having a night at home in front of the fire, or just simply actively doing something you love to do can help you feel self-love. When you do something you are good at, it can really boost your self-confidence, which in turn boosts your self-esteem.

3. Explore your spirituality. Spirituality teaches us things about ourselves that we never noticed before, such as our deepest thoughts, strongest passions, and our raw emotions. By exploring your spirituality, you are learning how to be the most authentic you while traveling down a journey that will help you stay focused on what you choose to believe in.

4. Stop comparing. When you see that other people are

starting a family or that someone is getting married, remember that they have their own problems too. Just because it looks like someone's life is perfect doesn't mean that it is. Everyone struggles, just like you. There is no one person who has a better lifestyle than others. Sure, you may not have graduated, or you may not be working at the career you love. Maybe you wish you had kids but can't have any. Maybe you have an illness, unlike most other people, and you become envious of their lives. Keep in mind that just because someone has a white picket fence, three kids, a happy marriage, and a well-trained dog doesn't mean they didn't struggle to get to where they are. Remember self-appreciation? This is the time that you need to be grateful for what you have. Know that you are worthy and strong enough to obtain whatever you want in life.

5. *Find your sanctuary.* Your sanctuary could be as creative as going to a place visually in your mind where you feel comfort and safety, or it could be a physical place in the universe. Think about a time that you felt most safe and most happy. Envision this place in your mind or go there physically. When you are there, let go of the other problems in your life. Just focus on this happy place without the extra stress or work pressure. This is how you can practice self-love at its finest.

6. *Chase your dreams.* A dream is a goal that someone tries to complete by the end of their life. Someone's dream could be that they surround themselves by animals on a large farm and live off the land. Another person's dream may be to become famous and known in the world for something. Most of the time, dreams do not get accomplished because we don't do anything to take a step toward it. Sit down and really figure out what your dream is, then work backward to how you can obtain it. When you are finished, you should see the steps on how to chase your dreams.

Self-love is about recognizing that you need love and that no one can give it to you. If you find that you fall into relationships too quickly or that you dive into work when you are stressed or that you don't give yourself enough time to think about what's most important to you, then you may need to practice these self-loving techniques. Remember that no one knows how to love you more than you do because you know how to love yourself the best. If you are struggling with finding ways to love yourself, take a step back and figure out how to show love to others. Most of the time, how we love someone else is how we want to be loved.

Transform from Who You Are to Who You Want to Be

Whether it's figuring out what you are most passionate about, developing a deeper sense of confidence, finding your true identity, or striving toward long-term goals, who you are now may not be who you want to be. As true self-appreciation means that you accept yourself fully for who you are and how you value yourself. It's also about building and growing every day. Here are ways you can truly break free of what's holding you back and strive to become who you have always wanted to be.

1. See yourself in a different light. You are a work of art, and the faster you understand this, the better off you will be. First, you need to accept who you are as an individual, then without judgment, figure out the things you want to work on the most. It's like a painter. As they paint, they take a step back and figure out what they can change and what they need to focus on. Look at yourself in this way and change something without the emotional attachment.

2. Find the associated habit to the thing that you want to change. You may struggle with changing what you want to change if it is linked or connected to a certain habit. First, you must figure out what this habit is, and start by changing that habit. It's like those gumdrops; you need to eat the candy around the gum before you can get to the gooey good part.

3. Set logical and reachable goals. Find something you want to change, like a smoking habit or a self-esteem issue. Start from the bottom and work your way up to changing it completely. If it's a self-esteem issue, then you are already in the right place. You just need to figure out where to start and what you will commit to every day to accomplish your small goals.

4. Surround yourself with genuine and authentic people. People who want the best for you and understand that you are solely working on yourself to change into who you want to be don't just say yes all the time. Authentic people really support you and give you constructive criticism. They listen and watch your progress so that they can challenge you and help you discover more about your personal growth.

If you truly want to change who you are, then dedicating yourself to this change is something that needs to be done every day. You must commit to the hard work and not give up when things become difficult. Be willing to take risks and accept that the future is untold. It's best to be able to manage change and be willing to adapt to it so that you can be more comfortable in striving further. The thing about becoming who you want to be is that it will not happen overnight. In fact, you may not even know or realize when the change happened. One day at a time will soon bring you to a day in the future that you can look back and appreciate all that you have done to this point.

Chapter Overview

Self-love is about learning to appreciate yourself through acceptance of who you are. By building on the foundation that you already have, you will start to realize that your personal confidence levels are slowly developing. When you think about self-love and appreciation, think of one or two things about yourself that you wouldn't give up for anything. Is it your attitude? Your looks? Behaviors or personality? Whatever it is, focus on that part of you. Be grateful that you have it because it is part of you that makes you unique. In the next chapter, we will talk about creating a plan so that you will always be able to develop self-confidence and self-esteem.

Chapter 8: Creating a Plan

Part of building confidence and self-esteem is changing your life. When you change your life, you must change your routine as well. When we start a new routine, it can be very difficult to stick to. To start a new ritual, you must learn how to develop new habits that turn into a routine. Most people find it easier to start with a morning routine, and then they gradually increase their routine into a full day, including nighttime. But the problem with creating a plan or learning to work with it is sticking to it to implement a change in your life. We are so used to doing what we have always done that our old habits start taking over our new ones if we aren't careful. When changing your habits and rituals, there are a few things to keep in mind during the process:

- Create a weekly reward for yourself for sticking to your new habitual routine.

- Reward yourself after every month for the progress you have made.

- Start small, doing one new thing at a time.

- Use a physical reminder to start practicing your new daily ritual, like leaving your running shoes on the toilet at night for when you wake up in the morning.

Here are a few more things you can do to stick to your new daily routine before we dive into actually creating one for self-esteem and confidence reasons:

1. *Link the new routine to the one you already have.* It is much easier to stick to something if you can connect it with something else. This is because our brains have been taught and trained one way that doing something completely new will set you up for more failures. If you want to practice getting more exercise in your schedule, include a morning stretch to your already habitual morning jog. If you like to journal, then add a schedule for this and create a routine for the next day to your journaling habit.

2. *Develop self-awareness.* When you develop self-awareness through being mindful of the present moment, it allows you to figure out why your past routines didn't work out. Mindfulness is about being present in every moment so that you can be more aware. Being more aware will help you recognize what is working and what is not. The best routine is one that you like and one that you have created to fit your specific needs. To increase your self-awareness, you need to ask yourself a few questions that will gain further insight into why you are changing your daily routine.

- What will this new life habit gain for you?

- What consequences or positive side effects will this new ritual have in your life?

- What will the outcome allow you to do or become?

- Which parts of your life will help support this new routine?

- How motivated are you to develop and stick to this routine?

Everything you plan to change in your life has to count and mean something. It has to be one thing at a time, and you should be able to see your efforts paying off in the long run. The new habits need to be thoroughly thought through in order for them not to fail. The problem with most people is that they read self-help books and dive right into the techniques they have read without putting much thought into the actual exercises. If you do this with a new habit or a new ritual, you may find that you aren't sticking to it a bit down the road. This can also be because what you are trying to do is conflicting with your life and already prioritized habits. If you start to notice that you are going back to your old ways, it may be in your best interest to start looking at why. This is where self-awareness comes into play so that you can realize it as it happens rather than when it's too late, and you have to start over.

3. Don't think too much into your late afternoon and evenings. For now, all you are focusing on is what to do in the morning that will set your day up for confidence and structure. The reason you must start with morning routines is that when we wake up in the morning, we seem to have so much more willpower and energy to get up and go. As the day goes on, the energy that we have in our brains starts to diminish. So make sure that when you do start your daily routine, you are starting as close as possible to when you wake up.

4. *Don't do it alone.* When doing something new, get your closest buddies in on it too. That way, when you wake up and don't feel like it one day, not only will you feel obligated to do it for your friends, but they will also encourage you to keep going. So maybe your friends don't want to live the same lifestyle as you, but maybe they want to get more exercise. Have a gym buddy. Have one friend for a healthy diet buddy, another friend for a positive reinforcement journaling buddy, and so on. When you include your friends, you gain more support, which will help you succeed in the long run.

Now when you make your confidence-boosting daily ritual, make a checklist so that you can check it off at the end of the day. Anything you missed, you can practice right then and there or set it up to do it tomorrow. Building confidence and self-esteem makes all the rest fall into place as they should. These things are self-respect, self-worth, self-appreciation, gratitude, awareness, etc.

Creating a Confidence Boosting Schedule

The thing about successful or confident people that you see or visit with is that they were not born that way. They worked hard at growing themselves and becoming who they want to be. You can do the same thing, too, with practice, dedication, and following the steps on how to keep a new daily routine. The one thing about confident people is that they know that when they procrastinate what needs to be done to work on themselves, they won't get anywhere or they will just drag themselves back even more.

Before you can start setting a schedule that works best for you, it's best to keep these things in mind to develop self-confidence and self-esteem.

1. Before anything else, get rid of the inner critic. The section "Fear of the Inner Critic" in chapter 6 explains how to get rid of the inner critic and how to talk back to your ANTs (automatic negative thoughts), and these ANTs are the most harmful thing that can slow your personal growth process down. If you struggle with an inner critic, then as soon as you get up, read over your critic journal (negative thought journal) and start rehearsing positive self-talk before you even leave the house. If you haven't already, then start planting sticky notes with positive quotes written on them around your house, especially in areas you can see them. More examples later in this chapter.

2. *Spend your downtime learning new things.* On your way to work, school, kids meeting, court, etc., learn new things. Studies have proven that when you learn something new outside of work, like a new language, new spiritual path, or math equations, your mental satisfaction boosts the same way a raise does. If you really want to see an increase in your confidence, listen to a language guide on the way to work, or play brain games for a bit of satisfaction and motivation to take on your day.

3. *Remember yourself.* Aside from the very busy morning routine that you are already planning and creating, put aside 10 to 15 minutes for yourself. This sets your mind to be refreshed and ready to go. Make sure it is you all by yourself—most likely before your shower or during a habit that you do alone, like getting dressed or using the washroom. Some exercises may include being mindful, telling yourself ten different things (different than yesterday) that you love about yourself, or writing in your gratitude journal. Once your mind is clear and you get out all the negative, you can start your day with a clear head and actually become more successful, as you have given yourself space to think.

4. *Get dressed up.* Occasionally, if not all the time, dress better than you would normally. Ditch the sweatpants or pajamas and put on some nice jeans and a button-up shirt. When you look good and feel like a professional, you will develop a more professional type of attitude. When others notice the change in your look and attitude, it can be a real confidence booster.

5. _Exercise._ Exercise has many benefits, including the increase in how you view yourself, which promotes self-esteem. It takes about twenty minutes for your body to get into the motion of exercise and about ten minutes after that to start feeling the effects. So if you start practicing a morning exercise ritual for up to thirty minutes, you will feel the positive effects on your body and mind. Exercise is one of the main key activities you can do to reduce stress and tension on the body.

6. _Don't worry about other people and what they think._ People are so worried about themselves and their own lives to worry too much about what's going on in your mind. Stop fortune-telling or dwelling on what you think others are thinking or saying about you. Chances are they aren't thinking much about you and your problems or paying much attention to how they feel about you. As depressing or shocking as this might sound, the truth is, when you don't care what others think and you only focus on your own opinion of yourself, your confidence levels will skyrocket.

Creating a full confidence-boosting morning routine will set the ball in motion for you to feel better about yourself. With this information, all that's left to do is figure out what type of routine you can create for yourself. As long as you get enough sleep, skip the snooze button, exercise, leave some alone time for yourself, and eat a well-balanced breakfast, you should feel more confident by the end of the month. It takes 21 days to create a routine and about 21 more days to stick to one so that you can develop a more regular daily habit and stick to it.

This is an example schedule:

- Get a good night's sleep.

- Wake up, exercise, or stretch (yoga).

- Eat a well-balanced breakfast.

- Shower, brush teeth, groom your hair, etc.

- Meditate or be with yourself.

- Read a book, journal, draw, or learn something new.

- Set up what needs to get done for your day.

- Implement positive self-talk/daily affirmations.

When you master your morning routine about whatever works for you, you can start figuring your nighttime routine, which is the reverse of your morning routine. While you end your morning routine with positive self-talk, during your nighttime routine, you do your positive self-talk right after journaling for what needs to be done tomorrow.

How to Create a Self-Love Routine

Self-confidence and self-esteem are important, but self-love is something that most people forget to do. You can work on your confidence, build your self-esteem, implement self-respect, and develop self-worth; however, if you don't learn to love yourself, then all that won't really matter at the end of the day. Self-love is like the glue that holds the positivity of self-improvement together. So now that you have created a self-boosting confidence morning ritual into your day, it's time to learn the next step, which is working a bit of self-love into your routine. Here is how:

1. Apply everything you use with purposeful love. When you lather lotion on your skin, really take the time to soak it up. Massage the essential oil into your skin or really focus on straightening your hair or gelling it with love. As you do this, think kind thoughts to yourself, such as "I am worthy," "I am special," "I look amazing," "I feel great," etc.

2. Every morning and night, say one thing to yourself that you love. This may be that you did really well in your interview today or that you were very helpful to your friend. You could say that you love that you are so empathetic or that you're grateful for your resilience. If you don't feel as great today, recognize what you inherited genetically from your parents and be happy that you got that trait or characteristic from them.

3. Create a schedule for right when you get home. Everyone needs to wind down, so it is only normal to turn the TV on or start dinner right away. However, instead of turning the TV on or before you make dinner right away, try making yourself your favorite cup of tea. Maybe you could change into something stylish and comfortable and cuddle up with your pet to have a "me time." Meditate for a moment because you deserve this for yourself after a long hard day at work.

4. End the day with appreciation. Maybe you had a bad day today—traffic jams, burned dinner, mistakes in the office, etc. Make sure you always end the day with what is positive in your life. This could be that your spouse is supportive and loving, your kids are healthy, or you have many good friends. Whatever you are appreciative for, make sure you write it down or tell someone about it. Who knows, you could make their night better too.

When you start acting on these to-dos, you will see that gradually you start feeling better about yourself. When you feel better, you feel positive and in control. One of the characteristics of a confident person is that they don't lack control in their lives. They know what they can't control, and they have learned to let go of it. What they can control is how to love themselves more every day. Don't wait to feel better and don't wait for people to lift you up or be supportive of you. Self-love is about doing what you want someone else to do for you, for yourself. So if you crave affection, lather that lotion. If you want compliments, tell yourself what you love most about yourself. If you need attention, sit with yourself and give your mind the thoughts it's been asking for. Over time, self-love will come.

How to Make Positive Flashcards for Everyday Use

It's time to get creative and make some flashcards. Flashcards come in handy for when you are having a tough day or a tough moment. It's for when everything doesn't seem to be working or that you just don't want to do your routine for today. It's okay to take a day off, but on those days, look at the flashcards you made. Make them in any color and use sparkles and gel pens to brighten it up. Here are some ideas you can put on your flashcards.

- By allowing myself to be happy, I can brighten someone else's day too.

- I have a great sense of humor that helps me get over these dark days.

- My spouse and I share a connection I won't take advantage of.

- I am a confident and well-deserving individual.

- I am resilient enough to tackle whatever life throws at me.

- I know I can achieve my goals because I am strong.

- I see fear as an opportunity, not as an obstacle.

- Today is the beginning of new successes to come my way.

- I am a problem solver.

- I am bold and confident.

- I always see the good in others because I am confident enough to know who supports me in my life.

- Nothing easy is worth my strength. I will tackle the difficult times because the reward is worth it.

- I am choosing to be proud of myself.

- I am worthy of great things in my life.

- I trust myself and my intuition to guide me to great things.

- My fight is not over.

- Life is happening right now.

- Breathe in peace. Breathe out drama and chaos.

- I will choose peace over war.

These are just a few positive affirmations. If you read these every day, your mood and attitude can change, and you can become the strong and confident individual you have strived so hard to be.

Here are some quotes about gratitude to put on your flashcards.

- "Learn to be thankful for what you have already, while you pursue all that you want" (Jim Rohn).

- "Be thankful for what you have; you'll end up having more. If you concentrate on what you don't have, you will never, ever have enough" (Oprah Winfrey).

- "Enjoy the little things, for one day you may look back and realize they were big things" (Robert Brault).

- "Some people complain that roses have thorns; I am grateful that thorns have roses" (Alphonse Karr).

- "The way to develop the best that is in a person is by appreciation and encouragement" (Charles Schwab).

You may choose to search for quotes or make up your own to make you feel better. The goal is to feel confident and strong. You can live vicariously through others' quotes and be one with your universe in what makes you who you are. Confidence and self-esteem are about learning how to practice self-love and gain self-respect. On those dark days, you accept that it's "one of those days" while also realizing that there are better days to come. The first step has to be taken by you, and it is up to you when you would like to start.

Chapter Overview

Routines are perhaps the most difficult thing to accomplish and stick to because we are so used to living our lives through what we know and what is familiar to us. However, you can choose to dive into changing your life around to become more confident and have a life that is more fulfilling. You can start by making simple habits to practice every day until it becomes a routine. Self-love comes from the soul. It is the glue that holds personal growth together. Without self-love, all the rest would be pieces of the puzzle that float around, trying to figure out where they belong. On those really tough days, flashcards about what makes you who you are and what makes you happy and grateful will get you through so that you can continue to stick with your daily rituals. Every so often, it is good to have a full "me day," but on those days, make sure you are making time to love yourself respectfully as well. In the next chapter, you can look forward to all the ways you can take care of yourself so that you can eventually fit these exercises into a full daytime schedule.

Chapter 9: Self-Care

Taking care of yourself is potentially the most important part of learning to be more confident and holding a high level of self-esteem. Many people think that taking care of themselves is just about providing their essential needs. That is not enough. Self-care is what we intentionally do to make sure that our minds (mental state), bodies (physical state), and spirits (emotional and soul-driven state) are balanced.

When you have a high anxiety level, your relationships are on the rocks, your brain is on overload, or you are overly stressed, it means that you have not taken good care of yourself. A good self-care routine means that you have taken enough time for yourself, you eat well-balanced meals, you exercise, you practice mindfulness to develop your mental awareness, and you have a load of supportive people in your life. When you eat well, you feed your body and your brain with the nutrients it needs to be alert and healthy. When you exercise, you shed the excess stress that builds up in your mind and body. When you meditate, you train yourself to become more relaxed and learn to let go of the small things that weigh you down. When you journal, you are also releasing energy and stress that you don't need. Finally, every individual needs affection, love, and support. When you surround yourself with positive and supportive people, you may feel a sense of inner peace and happiness as well that heals your soul and spiritual energy.

Many people have different definitions of what self-care is and how they should implement it into their lives, but in general, a checklist may help you understand more.

1. Say no to stress, which includes the following:

    o checking emails at night

    o attending social meet-ups just because you feel obligated to them

    o answering your phone when you know it's going to be an argument

    o not creating more drama than you already have

2. Learn to be assertive, which includes the following:

    o saying no to too many responsibilities

    o making too many promises that add to your plate

    o creating strong boundaries

    o standing up for yourself

3. Eat healthy, which includes the following:

    o adding all the essential vitamins and minerals into your diet

    o making sure your gut is healthy (the number-one reason for anxiety if stomach problems persist)

- eating balanced meals or small meals through the day

4. Get enough sleep, which includes the following:

   - having seven to eight hours of sleep every night

   - having no more than three hours of a nap during the day

   - waking up to the alarm without pressing the snooze button

5. Exercise, which includes the following:

   - learning yoga

   - doing healthy stretches before working out

   - not overdoing it

6. Make sure you are physically healthy, which includes the following:

   - checking in with the dentist

   - checking in with the doctor

   - making counseling appointments (if needed)

7. Spend time with people you love and care about, which includes the following:

   - having no distractions

- having a "me time"

- learning to give and take

8. Meditate, which includes the following:

  - finding time for just you

  - responding to your thoughts and challenging them

  - being mindful

  - practicing yoga

You have already learned to create an organized schedule and daily ritual in which you do every day. When you get used to your morning routine, make sure that you add the exercises throughout this chapter to get the highest benefits out of life. By making a schedule that you can fully take care of yourself while developing self-confidence, you may find that you generally become happier. This is because you are giving yourself more time to think, more time to focus, and overall more time for yourself.

Learn Meditation

Meditation has many benefits that include helping you center your mind, bringing your awareness onto yourself and your surroundings, and generally helping you relieve and manage stress. Meditation is where you learn to be one with your thoughts without judgment so that you can understand them better and reverse or promote them. Meditation is not the same as mindfulness, but it is very similar. Mindfulness is the practice of being fully aware and present in the given moment. At first, when you start practicing meditation and mindfulness, it can be difficult to get into it. Meditation, although easy, takes work, focus, and dedication as the more you do it, the better you will get at it. The trick is to be nonjudgmental. Do not beat yourself up if it doesn't work at first. If you continue to practice meditation, it will become easier, thus leaving you with incredible results that will make you feel mentally and emotionally better in the long run. Mindfulness meditation is to be used on a daily basis. It's like math. If you stop practicing, you will forget, and then it will be difficult to get back on track. Also, you will not see results right away.

Meditation, in general, is very useful, and mindfulness meditation is the most beneficial one. When we practice mindfulness, we develop the skills on how to return to and maintain the present moment. It takes three easy steps to get into meditation:

1. **Get comfortable.** Sit comfortably in a chair or lie down. Make sure that your posture is straight and your stomach is open for breathing. Notice your body, and do what feels the most comfortable for you. Close your eyes. Keep them focused on a focal point, and bring your attention to your breath.

2. **Focus on your breathing.** Don't try to control it. Just focus on where it's coming from. Is it coming from your nose or in your belly? Don't try to change the pace. Just notice your breath. Feel the sensation of your breath.

3. **Follow it for two minutes or more.** When you become distracted by your thoughts or you feel bored from the loud silence, be aware that this happened, and bring your attention back to your breath. If it helps, you can use a breathing ball exercise found on the Internet or in anxiety apps to bring your focus onto your breath. As the ball expands, you would take a breath. As it contracts, you would breathe out.

Once you finish your first session of this quick and simple exercise, you can now be curious about it. How long was it before you got distracted? Was your mind busy during the process? Was there something in particular you kept trying to think about? This is normal. Actually, this is what is supposed to happen because initially we are teaching ourselves to focus on the moment while being patient with our minds. When our minds wander, we become curious as to what needs the most attention. As we get better at learning to return our focus onto our breath, we can then learn to watch our thoughts and react to them appropriately. We must always finish the exercise with recentering our minds to our breaths and ending it on a positive note. If you feel as though you are getting stressed, that is when you would bring your focus back to the breath and patiently wait for yourself to calm down. These sessions can take anywhere between 5 and 30 minutes or more.

The Benefits of Exercise

Physical exercise helps you maintain stability and peace of mind. It helps you become physically healthier. Studies have recently proven that it helps you live longer as well. Exercise can combat diabetes, cardiovascular disease, and heart and lung problems. It is also beneficial to the health in the long term. Physical benefits of exercise include the following:

- weight management

- decreased risk of heart attack

- lower blood cholesterol levels

- decreased blood pressure

- development of stronger bones, muscles, and joints

- relief of muscle tensions

- boost in mood, energy, and relaxation

The benefits that exercise has on your mental health are as follows:

- helps with depression

- blocks the negative thoughts that distract you from daily activities

- increases social support if you exercise with a buddy

- improves sleep and the amount of rest you get

- increases healthy chemicals and decreases unhealthy chemicals in your brain, such as serotonin, endorphins, and stress hormones

It's good to aim for at least 30 minutes of exercise a day. You may notice, as you make exercise a routine, you feel hungrier. Choose foods that energize you rather than give you a sugar high until you crash. These foods are foods like green tea, eggs, protein, and green vegetables.

It doesn't matter which type of exercise you do. Just remember to never do the same exercise twice. For example, if you are toning your muscles one day, the next day, shoot for strengthening them. Each day, have a body group that you work on. For example, one day you work on your arms. Then give them a break the next day when you choose to work on your legs or stomach. The most beneficial exercise to practice is yoga.

What Is Yoga?

Yoga is a type of exercise that forces you to focus on your breathing techniques and on your mind. Not only does it have benefits on the body such as flexibility, strength building, and muscle toning, but it can affect your mind in positive ways too. Yoga is the practice of balance between your mind and body; and it reduces anxiety, depression, and stress. When you stretch or follow a video guide, you will mostly hear the tutor telling you to stretch, then breathe in, and hold it. As you release your stretch, release your breath. This type of workout helps you figure the difference between tensed muscles and strained muscles. It trains your brain that when you are stressed, you are more than likely tensed, so when you release the tension, you end up feeling a lot more relaxed. Although yoga may seem like a relaxed guided practice, it takes concentration and commitment to master it.

The benefits associated with yoga are as follows:

- tames and balances the mind

- combats negative emotions and thoughts

- promotes productivity and motivation

- brings peace of mind and welcomes clarity

- decreases stress

- reduces muscle inflammation

- improves heart health

- fights chronic pain

- increases sleep quality

- helps you become balanced physically, spiritually, and emotionally

- improves meditation practice as it helps you focus on breathing

- reduces headaches and migraines

- increases strength and resilience

By incorporating yoga into your daily routine, you may see positive side effects relating to your health, stress, and anxiety. Unlike other exercises, you will see and feel immediate benefits from it after a week of practicing.

Developing Better Socialization Skills

Studies have proven that healthy socialization promotes stronger and healthier individuals. This makes sense because when we look at people who are genuinely happy, they have a support system of people behind them. The old saying goes something like "It takes a village to raise a baby." This is true in all aspects. Whether you are only looking for help to overcome social anxiety or phobia or just looking to get out for a guys' night or a ladies' night. Friends and family are the people we turn to when we are sad, happy, angry, frustrated, etc. When we are in a good mood, we look for those to share our happiness with. When we are sad or upset, we look for our loved ones to vent to. Other benefits of socialization include the following:

- It relieves depression and anxiety symptoms.

- It builds a strong immune system due to the happiness we feel.

- You are able to focus and concentrate better.

  It boosts self-esteem and confidence.

- It reduces stress.

This is not a complete list, of course, but if you find that you are surrounded by negative people in your life, it's time to take a look at what type of friends you want to be around you. If you have negative friends who suck all your energy and you feel the opposite of these benefits, then there is a need to reevaluate the people around. Do you sometimes feel socially awkward in group settings or social events? That's maybe because you might be lacking effective communication skills. Here are some skills to work on if this feels like the case:

1. Listen. Turn off all distractions when you are being talked to. Make sure your phone is on silent, the TV isn't playing in the background, and your mind is centered on the person you are talking to. A lot of people hear what's being said to them without actually listening. This makes them unable to comprehend what is being said. A big reason as to why this happens is because we are in the technology age, and phones or other electronics become our main focus. In order to gain a better perspective and have closer relationships, be very aware of how you use your technology when visiting.

2. *Understand.* You don't have to fully understand something to be empathetic toward the opposing party; however, you do need to try to understand what is being said. When you listen with your full attention and rehearse what they have said back to you, you can gain a better understanding. When they feel as though you do acknowledge them, they will be more open and willing to hear you speak as well. People like to follow by example, so if you set a good example, you are portraying self-respect in what you wish to be done to you as well.

3. *Be empathetic.* When diving into conversations with people, oftentimes we think too fast, interrupt the other person, and don't fully get the concept of the interaction. If the other person is patient and empathetic, they will let you speak; however, they will leave the conversation feeling unsatisfied. Lead the whole interaction as empathetic to them as possible. Here are tips to be an empathetic communicator:

- Refrain from directing the conversation toward yourself.

- Do not try to interpret the other person's experiences.

- It's not a competition. Do *not* one-up the individual with your own experiences that seem better or worse than theirs.

- Do not dismiss the other's feelings as less than or say, "Don't be sad because . . ." and change the topic.

- Give them empathy; do not give sympathy.

4. Be responsible. If the other person has hurt your feelings in any way, bring this up to them but do not blame them for making you feel upset. Be responsible for your own actions and take credit for your own thoughts and feelings. They may have triggered the emotions, but they are not the cause of them. For example, rather than saying, "You are so unreliable, and for that, you have made me so angry," you could say, "I am upset with you because I was under the impression our agreements are promises we stick to. Can you please make sure this doesn't happen again?" The tone of the conversation will change if you are responsible rather than victimized.

5. Be careful with your body language. Communication is not all about words. Body language, such as facial expressions, tone of voice, and posture or gestures, are part of it too. When you are talking, make sure your body language matches what you are saying; otherwise, you could come off as confusing. Being confused or reading into mixed messages are never fun, and it might seem as though you are playing games, which can hurt your relationship.

Effective communication is key when building long-lasting love relationships. When you are heard, they understand. When they are heard, things go much smoother. When you ask for something from someone, make sure to use clear and concise language rather than beating around the bush. Someone is more likely to give you what you need when you are upfront and direct about it.

Chapter Overview

Meditation, yoga and exercise, eating healthy, and developing strong communication skills or closer relationships are all part of building self-esteem. When you work these things into your daily schedule, you can really start to feel more confident. Meditation is already one technique that follows suit with self-love and commitment to your inner character. Exercise makes you feel good, and developing good social habits works on your self-worth and respect. As you go through these many stages through developing a routine and putting them into your life, this is what it takes to be fully committed to personal growth.

Conclusion

You have now learned how to overcome your fears, practice a new routine, rid yourself of that evil inner critic, and develop ways to become more confident. It's your choice what you do with the information provided in this book, but go ahead and mark your favorite chapters and continue reading more to develop self-worth and individuality. Just remember that it's your life and you get to choose what you do with it. No matter what you choose to do, how you decide your journey from here, remember that self-confidence is not about defeating your negative thoughts but about knowing what you deserve. Self-esteem is about acting on what you deserve and going after what you want but having the confidence to do so. This self-confidence workbook teaches you self-love, positive affirmations, and meditation techniques because being who you are is important. Stop wasting time on people who do not support you and start supporting yourself through self-care and motivation. What matters is your own opinion.

The rest of your life starts right now, and it's entirely up to you what you are going to do with all the information you gathered in your life to this point.

Cheers!

References

AVS Mindfulness (2018). 5 incredible health benefits of face-to-face socialization. Retrieved from https://avsmindfulness.com/mindfulness/top-health-benefits-socialization/

Azab, M. (n.d.). The pain of worry: The anxious brain. Retrieved from https://www.psychologytoday.com/ca/blog/neuroscience-in-everyday-life/201811/the-pain-worry-the-anxious-brain

Better Health Channel (2012). Physical activity: It's important. Retrieved from https://www.betterhealth.vic.gov.au/health/healthyliving/physical-activity-its-important

Brandt, A. (2018). What do we mean by self-love?. Retrieved from https://abrandtherapy.com/what-do-we-mean-when-we-say-self-love/

Caiola, R. (2017). 8 ways to practice self-acceptance. Retrieved from https://www.huffpost.com/entry/8-ways-to-practice-self-acceptance_b_12640812

Chernoff, A. (2018). 10 truths that will change the way you see yourself today. Retrieved from http://www.marcandangel.com/2018/09/16/10-truths-that-will-change-the-way-you-see-yourself-today/

Cherry, K. (2019). Find out why self-esteem is important for success. Retrieved from https://www.verywellmind.com/what-is-self-esteem-2795868

Chopra, N. (2019). 10 wonderful ways to practice self-love. Retrieved from https://www.mindbodygreen.com/0-12428/10-wonderful-ways-to-practice-selflove.html

Cole, N. (2016). 8 powerful morning routines of ultra-confident people. Retrieved from https://www.inc.com/elle-kaplan/8-powerful-morning-routines-of-ultra-confident-people.html

Cole, N. (2016). Steps to transforming yourself from who you are to who you want to be. Retrieved from https://www.inc.com/nicolas-cole/7-steps-to-transform-yourself-from-who-you-are-to-who-you-want-to-be.html

Cooper, B. B. (2018). How to think positive every day: 4 simple steps to a happier life. Retrieved from https://open.buffer.com/think-positive/

Corelli, R. (2017). Thoughts affect feelings, feelings affect actions, actions determine happiness. Retrieved from https://www.theodysseyonline.com/thoughts-effect-feelings-feelings-effect-actions-actions-determine-happiness

Daskal, L. (2015). Confident ways to overcome your shyness. Retrieved from https://www.inc.com/lolly-daskal/13-confident-ways-to-overcome-your-shyness.html

Edison, T. (2016). Power of confidence: 7 characteristics of a

confident person. Retrieved from
https://www.toptierleadership.com/blog/power-of-confidence-7-characteristics-of-a-confident-person/

Florence, J. (2017). Building confidence and self-esteem. Retrieved from https://www.huffpost.com/entry/building-confidence-and-s_b_6111172?guccounter=1

Fonvielle, D. (n.d.). What is self-confidence about?. Retrieved from http://www.alwaysgreater.com/achievements/what-does-self-confidence-mean-to-you

Fonvielle, D. (n.d.). Why is confidence important in life?. Retrieved from http://www.alwaysgreater.com/achievements/why-is-self-confidence-important-benefits-of-self-confidence

GoodTherapy.org (2018). Does your inner critic fuel anxiety? What can you learn instead?. Retrieved from https://www.goodtherapy.org/blog/does-your-inner critic-fuel-anxiety-what-can-you-learn-instead-0525185

Greenberg, M. (n.d.). Changing your brain by changing your mind. Retrieved from https://www.psychologytoday.com/us/blog/the-mindful-self-express/201109/changing-your-brain-changing-your-mind

Haden, J. (2014). 9 qualities of remarkably confident people. Retrieved from https://www.inc.com/jeff-haden/9-qualities-of-remarkably-confident-people-th.html

Iannarino, A. (2018). 10 negative mindset infections that destroy success. Retrieved from https://thesalesblog.com/2018/06/23/10-negative-mindset-infections-that-destroy-success/

Khoshaba, D. (n.d.). A seven-step prescription for self-love. Retrieved from https://www.psychologytoday.com/ca/blog/get-hardy/201203/seven-step-prescription-self-love

Kingsnorth, L. (n.d.). 10 tips for effective communication. Retrieved from http://www.dailygood.org/story/1366/10-tips-for-effective-communication-liz-kingsnorth/

Krissy Brady. (2019). How to understand yourself. Retrieved from https://www.lifehack.org/articles/communication/25-questions-help-you-understand-yourself-and-unlock-your-potential.html

Legg, T. (n.d.) Anxiety: Causes, symptoms, treatment, and more. Retrieved from https://www.healthline.com/health/anxiety#natural-remedies

Link, R. (n.d.) 13 benefits of yoga that are supported by science. Retrieved from https://www.healthline.com/nutrition/13-benefits-of-yoga#section14

McLoughlin, R. (n.d.). 5 little self-love routines that just might change your life. Retrieved from http://rebeccamcloughlin.com/2015/04/04/5-little-self-love-routines-that-just-might-change-your-life/

Mindful Staff (2019). How to meditate. Retrieved from
https://www.mindful.org/how-to-meditate/

Nerdy Creator (2019). Why do you need to be thankful and how
to do it? Retrieved from
https://www.nerdycreator.com/blog/self-appreciation-
meaning/

Newman, T. (2018). Fear: What happens in the brain and
body?. Retrieved from
https://www.medicalnewstoday.com/articles/323492.php

PsychAlive (2014, May 09). The importance of self-worth.
Retrieved from https://www.psychalive.org/self-worth/

PsychAlive (2017, March 13). 4 steps to conquer your inner
critic. Retrieved from https://www.psychalive.org/4-steps-to-
conquer-your-inner critic/

PsychAlive (2018, April 02). The critical inner voice explained.
Retrieved from https://www.psychalive.org/critical-inner-
voice/

Psychology Today (n.d.). Self-esteem. Retrieved from
https://www.psychologytoday.com/ca/basics/self-esteem

Razzetti, G. (2018). Self-appreciation is the foundation of life.
Retrieved from https://medium.com/personal-growth/self-
appreciation-is-the-foundation-of-life-c44af9189040

Roberts, E. (n.d.). The difference between self-esteem and self-
confidence. Retrieved from

https://www.healthyplace.com/blogs/buildingselfesteem/2012/05/the-difference-between-self-esteem-and-self-confidence

Sasson, R. (n.d.). Self-acceptance: What is it? Retrieved from https://www.successconsciousness.com/self-acceptance.htm

Shallard, P. (2019). How to make yourself stick to a routine. Retrieved from https://www.commitaction.com/how-to-stick-to-a-routine/

Smith, E. M. (n.d.). What is positivity? The definition may surprise you. Retrieved from https://www.healthyplace.com/self-help/positivity/what-is-positivity-the-definition-may-surprise-you

Sol, M. (2019). 13 signs it's time to build some goddamn self-respect. Retrieved from https://lonerwolf.com/self-respect/

Sweatt, L. (2018). Success: 15 thoughtful quotes about gratitude. Retrieved from https://www.success.com/15-thoughtful-quotes-about-gratitude/

Winch, G. (n.d.). 10 signs that you might have fear of failure. Retrieved from https://www.psychologytoday.com/ca/blog/the-squeaky-wheel/201306/10-signs-you-might-have-fear-failure